Table of Contents

I. Dedication 2

II. Acknowledgment 4

Chapter 1: Introduction 5

    1. When was I first called David? 11

    2. Mother of David 15

    3. Jesus is God of gods and Lord of lords. 29

Chapter 2. The promises to King David, my own blessings! 36

Chapter 3. Promises of David in action in me. 47

    1. Miraculous healing of my mother with her cancer............................ 48

    2. Saved when I cried out:"Save your king oh God!" 53

    3. To change a rule that was against my right at University: The spirit of David took over me. 57

    4. The challenge to resuscitate a dying baby 68

    5. Miraculous rise of the price of Bitcoin 82

    6. The power through the name of the Lord Jesus Christ 99

        1. The end of Osama Ben Laden 101

        2. The victory of Mr Donald Trump in the US general presidential elections. 104

Chapter 4. What men of God said about directly or not. 128

Chapter 5: Rule nations to fulfill the great commission easily 144

Chapter 6. The World kingdom called "Bethel", a holy nation under one God Jesus Christ and me his King David. 149

I. Dedication

I dedicate this book to all the people who died due to terrorist attack in September, 11th September, 2001 as known as 9/11 in the United States of America. They were people from different nationalities.

I would like also to dedicate this book to Jews killed during the Second World War. They were wonderful people who deserved to live long and help to beautify the world. May God bless my beloved and great people of Germany who fought against that hatred. I love Israel and Germany!

I would like also to dedicate my book to all unborn babies killed by their parents while in the womb sometimes helped by some health workers like me. Why do they not stop their own heart but put an end to those beautiful Human beings? Because they are stronger than those babies? Time has come to change any form of injustice all over the world.

I cannot forget to dedicate this book to wonderful men, women and children killed in Rwanda in 1994 because they were Tutsi. The whole world needed to benefit their talents and different gifts that God had given them. This book is dedicated to everyone killed in Rwanda, Burundi because they were Tutsi or Hutu. I love you Burundi and Rwanda!

I cannot forget to dedicate my book to the late great man Abraham Lincoln, the former US president who abolished slavery between brothers and sisters human beings but in different skin color. May his soul rest in peace!

This dedication goes to Dr Martin Luther King and all my beloved great people of America for having rejected segregation between black and white and chose to live in America as one people. I love you America!

This unifying project is dedicated also to the my beloved great people of South Africa especially to the late ex president of South Africa Nelson Mandela for his the people of the late great man Nelson Mandela because chose unity and love between them as one people instead of using revenge against his the people who practiced apartheid. I love you South Africa!

I dedicate this great and wonderful project to all my family and all beloved and great people of Burundi.

To the Pentecostal church of Burundi and to all the body of Christ from all over the world, to my beloved and great people of Sweden for sending missionaries founders of our church in Burundi, Congo and Rwanda at the risk of their lives, I dedicate this wonderful book;

I dedicate this book to all missionaries from all over the world who take the gospel to different areas of the world sometimes at the risk of their lives.

To my beloved and great people of Zambia, I dedicate also this book because Zambia has dared to declare the nation as a "Christian nation". God bless all the nation of Zambia with lasting prosperity, peace and righteousness of Christ Jesus! I love you Zambia!

I would like to extend my dedication to United Nations, a global organization that tries to make sure there is peace in the world!

Finally, I dedicate this book to every human being from all over the world that God brought to stay on our beautiful planet and every place where life is possible in the universe. I love you everybody wherever you are! I am proud of everyone and all the creation! Let us be one people loving each other pushing one another to the prosperity, peace, good health and make the whole world one nation, one great people!

II. Acknowledgment

Firstly, I would like to acknowledge my heavenly Father who gives me strength and oxygen I need for my existence for me to able to write this book.

I thank with all my heart Jesus Christ the good savior of Humanity for having accepted willingly to suffer for me and for all nations of all generations till death in order to save His beloved Humanity. I am writing this book because He died for me and revealed himself to me. I am a son of God enjoying the blessings of David because of Jesus. The Rock of my salvation has given me access to the promises of God by and for Himself. I am now a son of God, a son of Abraham a son of David through Christ Jesus.

My acknowledgment goes equally for my late mother who did not abandon me and abort me due to the pain she experienced during all the period of my conception. She chose to be patient despise the pain she had to undergo on the day of my birth as her firstborn.

I thank so much my beloved biological father who has been caring well his noble duty as a "father". He and my late mother raised me in the fear of God. May God bless and strengthen him and give him to live long and always full of the Holy Spirit and the heart that loves God.

Finally, I would like to thank all who helped directly or indirectly like Jesus anointed Ministries international, Wells of salvation ministry like Apostle Levi Nyirongo, Pastor Agatha Mulenga, Pastor Lawrence Nkonde and so on to make this project possible. I love and thank everybody who helped me like Evangelist Mutungwa, Dr Sakufiwa for the realization of this amazing book. Thanks for my dear sister in the Lord Hoori Khandani and Reverend Solomon Lomotey for their constructive advice concerning this book.

May the Lord Jesus Christ bless you all abundantly according to His promise to make those who help me succeed along with your families and people and cause you to live long with a wonderful good health!

Chapter 1: Introduction

I am a medical doctor born in Burundi, my beloved and great nation located in Africa specifically in East Africa.

After my birth at hospital, my dearest father was asked what name he wanted me to be called. He said:"**Nizigiyimana**" meaning" **In God we trust** ".

In other words, I was cast on God the creator of Heaven and the earth since my birthday. Hope you understand why I love the great people of America because of their "**In God we trust**" slogan . I cerebrate what the supreme court ruled against people who wanted to remove that in different places.

 Burundi has an ethnical issue -like hatred between my beloved great people Hutu and my beloved great people Tutsi- that had been pulling down the country for many years instead of going forward.

I thank God I have been protected from being under influence of stereotypes against my different ethnical people.

The great Burundi has three (3) different types of people called:" Hutu, Tutsi and Twa." They are all great. I love my father and mother because they never talked to me about Hutu people as my enemies. His friends are Hutu and Tutsi. I grew up in that atmosphere of loving all people including the great people who used to be neglected in Burundi, my beloved and great people of Twa. Whether minority or majority we are all one people that must live together as one great nation one Burundi.

At university there were two (2) blocks of Hutu and Tutsi. Tutsi students would find themselves almost alone without Hutu and so Hutu students would find themselves almost alone without Tutsi among them.

You know what? I would go among the Hutu students and make them my friend and they were always asking me:" Who are you? I am a child of God. Maybe when they looked at me they could see me looking like Tutsi but they were confused because I was always with them some time and some time with Tutsi students. I am proud of that behavior.

A human being is a human being! I have to love everybody! Why hating a human being like you? Why not desiring to see other people doing well like you? When you practice love you are promoting yourself!

I used to say to myself I am Hutu, I am Tutsi, I am TWA. All of them are my beloved people and I am proud of that. I stayed in a house with Hutu people my people. One of them I used to call her as my "mother." That great woman of God but late now used to take care of me like her beloved son. She was a woman who loved to help people. Her husband -who used to beat her because she was not giving birth to male children- before he passed away, used to call her "UNHCR **United Nations High Commissioner for Refugees**." because she was helping everyone. And the more she helps other people the more God continued to make her richer. I thank God for having given her later a son, who came as a "savior" to her against the unfounded hate of her husband.

One day that mother wanted to pay for me the school fees at a private university but I did not get a place and continued at the public University called "the University of Burundi." She was ready for anything that can make me happy. Her children are like my sisters and my brother. You see how blessed I was? God can use a very person for your goodness that is why it is not good to despise other people. You do not know who has been ordained to take you to your destination. That is a secret of God unless it is revealed unto you. There is a reason why you are with someone together for the first time or many times, be grateful for that and talk to each other nicely.

Therefore, stop limiting yourself and lock up to yourself in your small tribe, race, nation... Start seeing yourself as a world citizen. No matter how rich your nation maybe it is not a reason to cut relationship with so called poor nations as long as they are human beings like you. They have hands you may need ; therefore look how you can help them to get developed like you because you will find that you are making yourself more developed and more richer.

Today in Zambia the people that are strengthening me or blessing me are not Burundians or members of my family but they are people of this wonderful nation of Zambia. Be thankful to God for who you are and be grateful to God also for your brothers and sisters who are black or white because God created people with different skin colors for your own good and happiness. Love everyone!

My prayer is to see *One Rwanda one People*" and one *Burundi one Nation* like what my beloved and great people of Zambia a great nation with more than 73 tribes did as *"One Zambia one Nation."*

Imagine if we form one nation great nation where all nations from all over the world are found themselves and use English **as an official language** just to unite all the nations under one King and always before the news we hear **"One world one nation"** like in my great beloved people of Zambia. Imagine if we are united as one powerful nation through ties of love to each other and make great our great world nation! Only in this way we are going to overcome poverty and wars between nations because there will be no more of "this is my territory, this is our water". There will be no need of nuclear weapon that my beloved and great people of Iran and North Korea are trying by all means to possess like other powerful nations.

My beloved and great people of China, Russia and United States of America will be working together as one people with the entire whole world developing all together including my beloved and great people of Africa. Those trillions of US dollars we are spending in military will be spent against poverty. There will be no space war at all because the space belongs to all of us. Why fight for the things we did not create?

Zambia is not ashamed in their tribes. It is an easy thing to ask a tribe of a Zambian which is not easy in Burundi or Rwanda. When I see people who resemble Tutsi or Hutu in Burundi or Rwanda in Zambian people and they do not hate each other because their noise like in Burundi or Rwanda.

If in Zambia they cannot hate and kill each other because of their noise why not stop that stupidity of killing each other for generations in Burundi and Rwanda forever and build a strong nation without any hatred based on the appearance of somebody's noise. Enough is enough!

Forget the killing in the past and come together and form one strong new Burundi one people and one strong new Rwanda, one people. ***Choose forgiveness and love one another.***

I do not like to be in one box. Every human being is my friend my brother, my sister. Black, White, Chinese, people Asiatic… as long as they are human beings I love them and they are my people. They can feel hungry like me, they can be happy like me therefore we as human beings are one and must live together as one and help each other as one world great nation without borders. A world without egoism. A world that shares technology easily with other nations because we are all human beings condemned to better our lives with dignity.

At university, one of my friends was a Hutu and very intelligent, Hutu people have been into power for many years in Burundi.

If you want to overcome some of stereotypes you have accepted effortlessly because of what you heard against other people from your different leaders or ancestors, it is easy and you will always find that what you were told is a fake information and that there is no reason of hating each other.

I remember when I took oath as a medical doctor in Burundi, I held the Burundian flag by faith as a "world flag". All nations are my people. I am a medical doctor for all nations and I am proud of that.

I like to watch news not of the local news but also international news. Why? I want to know what is happening around the globe. I am concerned of what happening around the globe and think what can be done as solution to different issues. Today God has made our world too small to live without knowing what happening around the globe almost instantly. We are in the right time of gathering all nations of our beautiful world into one great nation.

A friend of mine asked me one day why I like to watch those international news through these great main media like CNN, FOX news, France 24; Aljazeera... where they show almost only the bad news. "I want to know what is happening around the world with my people from all over the world so that I can pray for them." I replied to her. I believe prayer is powerful because God does perform miracles through prayers!

"Why have you come to work at our clinic? Is it not to wait for the patients who are coming with their health issues and give a solution for them to come out of their bad conditions?" I asked her again. She kept quiet like someone convinced.

People should not fear to watch news nationally and internationally for them to be a solution to the different people of our beloved and great world. You can pray for any problem that is emerging in any part of the world and bring a change. And the Father in heaven who sees in secret will reward you! The time will never allow you to be isolationist! What is hitting in South Arabia is also hitting the global economy. As the whole world, we form one body, it Hurricane is hitting America it is also hitting the whole body: The whole world!

1. When was I first called David?

When I was 11 years old, I was given a new name in my local Pentecostal church in an area called Kibenga right in the Capital city of Bujumbura. What's that?"**David**" was the new name given to me. Jesus says "**I tell you the truth, whatever you forbid on earth will be forbidden in heaven, and whatever you permit on earth will be permitted in heaven.**" Matthew 18:18, New Living Translation.

So that name given in my great church was also permitted in heaven.

A certain Sunday that I will never forget I asked one of the leaders to give a time to testify how I got born again. As small as I was, the pulpit was taller than me then they had to put me on the drum for me to be able to speak facing the audience holding the microphone in my hands. At the end of my testimony, a man of God who was leading said:" You are David".

The church started calling me "**David**". In other words, the man of God said you are like David the one who fought against Goliath in the name of the Lord Yahweh and won using a stone and a slinger without a sword in his hands.

David cut off his head and later on became a king after the heart of God over the Israel who was the people of God in all the Earth before Jesus died for all nations for all generations. Hope you understand why I love the people of Israel as my own people and Arabs people because they share one ancestor "Abraham".

These great people they are brothers. They must love each other between themselves and between them and all Christians because all the people became children of Abraham through our dearest Jesus the MESSIAH! Whether you believe it or not you cannot change it. A car is a car whether you believe it or not!

While at University in the medical faculty, I put on that name of "DAVID" cheerfully and wholeheartedly. I received the spirit of David I said to my God who is the Father of the Whole World:" *Heavenly Father may you use me seven times the same way you used King David in his time in the name of Jesus Christ but protect me from the weakness of King David and those of King Solomon. I want to make a difference! Both King David and King Solomon did something that gave occasion to the enemies of the LORD to blaspheme. I even told the Lord to make me wiser and wealthier than King Solomon and keep me from doing wrong against his laws. I want to shame the devil. In short, I want to please my Lord Jesus Christ by making a difference. I want to be a rich king through holy ways and still love God and His people as a husband of one wife. I want badly to change what King Solomon did. I give myself to you Lord*

Jesus to rule like your king David over all nations because you died for all nations without exception of any nation around the globe in your name of Jesus Christ!"

I started reading the bible to know who was David whose name means **"beloved"**.

As, I was reading the bible I found out that the same way I was cast to the Lord and pushed to trust in God through my surname from my mother's breast, King David also was pushed to trust in the Lord since his mother's breast: *"Yet you brought me out of the womb; you made me trust in you, even at my mother's breast. From birth I was cast on you; from my mother's womb you have been my God."***Psalm22:10, New International Version (NIV).**

Why this resemblance? I always ask myself. Simple c ISBN: 9781701087231 oincidence? I know that nothing happen by accident.

Another resemblance with King David: When my mother was still alive, she is the one who used to share the word of God at home. She would organize how to pray. She was committed in serving the Lord. She used to sing in a choir and she liked that so much. I used to escort her when she was going to visit different people at their place and share the Word of God with them. She was my really my friend and I loved her a lot.

The way I was too closed to my mother was the same connection that King David had with his mother. How I know that?

That is very simple question because King David said:"***Truly I am your servant, LORD; I serve you just as my mother did; you have freed me from my chains.*** " Psalm 116Psalm116:16, New **International Version.**

That means that King David was most connected to his mother than to his father. The bible does not tell us about the mother of David. Why David was the person behind the sheep of his father? Why the father forgot about him when the prophet of the Yahweh came to anoint one of his sons to become king of Israel to unseat king Saul?

I used to wonder why until I read the following article about the mother of King David by this great woman **Chana Weisberg**.

One world one nation under one God, Jesus Christ

2. Mother of David

Save me, O God, for the waters threaten to engulf me . . .

I am wearied by my calling out, and my throat is dry. I've lost hope in waiting . . .

More numerous than the hairs on my head are those who hate me without reason . . .

Must I then repay what I have not stolen?

Mighty are those who would cut me down, who are my enemies without cause . . .

O God, You know my folly, and my unintended wrongs are not hidden from You . . .

It is for Your sake that I have borne disgrace, that humiliation covers my face.

I have become a stranger to my brothers, an alien to my mother's sons.

Out of envy for Your House, they ravaged me; the disgraces of those who revile You have fallen upon me . . .

Those who sit by the gate talk about me. I am the taunt of drunkards . . .

Disgrace breaks my heart, and I am left deathly sick.

I hope for solace, but there is none; and for someone to comfort me, but I find no one.

They put gall into my meal, and give me vinegar to quench my thirst . . . (Psalm 69)[1]

This psalm describes the life of a poor, despised and lowly individual, who lacks even a single friend to comfort him. It is the voice of a tormented soul who has experienced untold humiliation and disgrace. Through no apparent cause of his own, he is surrounded by enemies who wish to cut him down; even his own brothers are strangers to him, ravaging and reviling him.

Amazingly, this is the voice of the mighty King David, righteous and beloved servant of God, feared and awed by all.

King David had many challenges throughout his life. But at what point did this great individual feel so alone, so disgraced, and so undeserving of love and friendship?

What caused King David to face such an intense ignominy, to be shunned by his own brothers in his home ("I have become a stranger to my brothers"), by the Torah sages who sat in judgment at the gates ("those who sit by the gate talk about me") and by the drunkards on the street corners ("I am the taunt of drunkards")? What had King David done to arouse such ire and contempt? And was there no one, at this time in his life, which would provide him with love, comfort and friendship?

This psalm, in which King David passionately gives voice to the heaviest burdens of his soul, refers to a period of twenty-eight years, from his earliest childhood until he was coronated as king of the people of Israel by the prophet Samuel.

David was born into the illustrious family of Yishai (Jesse), who served as the head of the *Sanhedrin* (supreme court of Torah law), and was one of the most distinguished leaders of his generation. Yishai was a man of such greatness that the Talmud (Shabbat 55b) observes that "Yishai was one of only four righteous individuals who died solely due to the instigation of the serpent"—i.e., only because death was decreed upon the human race when Adam and Eve ate from the Tree of Knowledge at the serpent's instigation, not due to any sin or flaw of his own. David was the youngest in his family, which included seven other illustrious and charismatic brothers.

Yet, when David was born, this prominent family greeted his birth with utter derision and contempt. As David describes quite literally in the psalm, "I was a stranger to my brothers, a foreigner to my mother's sons. . . they put gall in my meal, and gave me vinegar to quench my thirst."

David was not permitted to eat with the rest of his family, but was assigned to a separate table in the corner. He was given the task of shepherd because "they hoped that a wild beast would come and kill him while he was performing his duties,"[2] and for this reason was sent to pasture in dangerous areas full of lions and bears.[3]

Only one individual throughout David's youth was pained by his unjustified plight, and felt a deep and unconditional bond of love for the child whom she alone knew was undoubtedly pure.

This was King David's mother, Nitzevet bat Adael, who felt the intensity of her youngest child's pain and rejection as her own.

Torn and anguished by David's unwarranted degradation, yet powerless to stop it, Nitzevet stood by the sidelines, in solidarity with him, shunned herself, as she too cried rivers of tears, awaiting the time when justice would be served. It would take twenty-eight long years of assault and rejection, suffering and degradation until that justice would finally begin to materialize.

David's Birth

Why was the young David so reviled by his brothers and people?

To understand the hatred directed toward David, we need to investigate the inner workings behind the events, the secret episodes that aren't recorded in the prophetic books but are alluded to in Midrashim.[4]

David's father, Yishai, was the grandson of Boaz and Ruth. After several years of marriage to his wife, Nitzevet, and after having raised several virtuous children, Yishai began to entertain personal doubts about his ancestry. True, he was the leading Torah authority of his day, but his grandmother Ruth was a convert from the nation of Moab, as related in the book of Ruth.

During Ruth's lifetime, many individuals were doubtful about the legitimacy of her marriage to Boaz. The Torah specifically forbids an Israelite to marry a Moabite convert, since this is the nation that cruelly refused the Jewish people passage through their land, or food and drink to purchase, when they wandered in the desert after being freed from Egypt.

Boaz and the sages understood this law—as per the classic interpretation transmitted in the "Oral Torah"—as forbidding intermarriage with converted *male* Moabites (who were the ones responsible for the cruel conduct), while exempting female Moabite converts. With his marriage to Ruth, Boaz hoped to clarify and publicize this Torah law, which was still unknown to the masses.

Boaz died the night after his marriage with Ruth. Ruth had conceived and subsequently gave birth to their son Oved, the father of Yishai. Some rabble-rousers at the time claimed that Boaz's death verified that his marriage to Ruth the Moabite had indeed been forbidden.

Time would prove differently. Once Oved (so called because he was a true *oved*, servant of God), and later Yishai and his offspring, were born, their righteous conduct and prestigious positions proved the legitimacy of their ancestry. It was impossible that men of such caliber could have descended from a forbidden union.

However, later in his life, doubt gripped at Yishai's heart, gnawing away at the very foundation of his existence. Being the sincere individual that he was, his integrity compelled him to action.

If Yishai's status was questionable, he was not permitted to remain married to his wife, a veritable Israelite. Disregarding the personal sacrifice, Yishai decided the only solution would be to separate from her, no longer engaging in marital relations. Yishai's children were aware of this separation.

After a number of years had passed, Yishai longed for a child whose ancestry would be unquestionable. His plan was to engage in relations with his Canaanite maidservant.

He said to her: "I will be freeing you conditionally. If my status as a Jew is legitimate, then you are freed as a proper Jewish convert to marry me. If, however, my status is blemished and I have the legal status of a Moabite convert forbidden to marry an Israelite, I am not giving you your freedom; but as a *shifchah k'naanit*, a Canaanite maidservant, you may marry a Moabite convert."

The maidservant was aware of the anguish of her mistress, Nitzevet. She understood her pain in being separated from her husband for so many years. She knew, as well, of Nitzevet's longing for more children.

The empathetic maidservant secretly approached Nitzevet and informed her of Yishai's plan, suggesting a bold counterplan.

"Let us learn from your ancestresses and replicate their actions. Switch places with me tonight, just as Leah did with Rachel," she advised.

With a prayer on her lips that her plan succeeds, Nitzevet took the place of her maidservant. That night, Nitzevet conceived. Yishai remained unaware of the switch.

After three months, Nitzevet's pregnancy became obvious. Incensed, her sons wished to kill their apparently adulterous mother and the "illegitimate" fetus that she carried. Nitzevet, for her part, would not embarrass her husband by revealing the truth of what had occurred. Like her ancestress Tamar, who was prepared to be burned alive rather than embarrass Judah,[5] Nitzevet chose a vow of silence. And like Tamar, Nitzevet would be rewarded for her silence with a child of greatness who would be the forebear of Moshiach.

Unaware of the truth behind his wife's pregnancy, but having compassion on her, Yishai ordered his sons not to touch her. "Do not kill her! Instead, let the child that will be born be treated as a lowly and despised servant. In this way everyone will realize that his status is questionable and, as an illegitimate child, he will not marry an Israelite."

From the time of his birth onwards, then, Nitzevet's son was treated by his brothers as an abominable outcast.[6] Noting the conduct of his brothers, the rest of the community assumed that this youth was a treacherous sinner full of unspeakable guilt.

On the infrequent occasions that Nitzevet's son would return from the pastures to his home in Beit Lechem (Bethlehem), he was shunned by the townspeople. If something was lost or stolen, he was accused as the natural culprit, and ordered, in the words of the psalm, to "repay what I have not stolen."

Eventually, the entire lineage of Yishai was questioned, as well as the basis of the original law of the Moabite convert. People claimed that all the positive qualities of Boaz became manifest in Yishai and his illustrious seven sons, while all the negative character traits from Ruth the Moabite clung to this despicable youngest son.

Anointing King David

We are first introduced to David when the prophet Samuel is commanded to go to Beit Lechem to anoint a new king, to replace the rejected King Saul.

Samuel arrives in Beit Lechem, and the elders of the city come out to greet him, nervous at this unusual and unexpected visit, since the elderly prophet had stopped circulating throughout the land. The elders feared that Samuel had heard about a grievous sin that was taking place in their city.[7] Perhaps he had come to rebuke them over the behavior of Yishai's despised shepherd boy, living in their midst.

Samuel declared, however, that he had come in peace, and asked the elders, and Yishai and his sons, to join him for a sacrificial feast. As an elder, it was natural for Yishai to be invited; but when his sons were inexplicably also invited, they worried that perhaps the prophet had come to publicly reveal the embarrassing and illegitimate origins of their brother. Unbeknownst to them, Samuel would anoint the new king of Israel at this feast. All that had been revealed to the prophet at this point was that the new king would be a son of Yishai.

When they came, Samuel saw Eliav (Yishai's oldest son), and he thought, "Surely God's anointed stands before Him!"

But God said to Samuel, "Don't look at his appearance or his great height, for I have rejected him. God does not see with mere eyes, like a man does. God sees the heart!"

Then Yishai called Avinadav (his second son), and made him pass before Samuel. He said: "God did not choose this one either."

Yishai made Shammah pass, and Samuel said, "God has not chosen this one either."

Yishai had his seven sons pass before Samuel. Samuel said to Yishai, "God has not chosen any of them."

At last Samuel said to Yishai, "Are there no lads remaining?"

He answered, "A small one is left; he is taking care of the sheep."

So Samuel said to him, "Send for him and have him brought; we will not stir until he comes here."

So he sent for him and had him brought. He was of ruddy complexion with red hair, beautiful eyes, and handsome to look at.

God said: "Rise up, anoint him, for this is the one!" (**I Samuel 16:6**–12)

The Small One, Left Behind

As Samuel laid his eyes on Yishai's eldest son, he was certain that this was the future king of Israel. Tall, handsome and distinguished, Eliav was the one whom Samuel was ready to anoint, until God reprimanded Samuel to look not at the outside but at the inside.[8]

No longer did Samuel make any assumptions of his own, but he waited to be told who was to become the next king. All the seven sons of Yishai had passed before Samuel, and none of them had been chosen.

"Are these all the lads?" Samuel asked. Samuel prophetically chose his words carefully. Had he asked if these were all Yishai's *sons*, Yishai would have answered affirmatively, that there were no more of *his sons*, since David was not given the status of a son?

Instead, Yishai answered, "A small one is left; he is taking care of the sheep." David's status was small in Yishai's eyes. He was hoping that Samuel would allow David to remain where he was, out of trouble, tending to the sheep in the faraway pastures.

But Samuel ordered that David immediately be summoned to the feast. A messenger was dispatched to David who, out of respect for the prophet, first went home to wash himself and change his clothes. Unaccustomed to seeing David home at such a time, Nitzevet inquired, "Why did you come home in the middle of the day?"

David explained the reason, and Nitzevet answered, "If so, I too am accompanying you."

As David arrived, Samuel saw a man "of ruddy complexion, with red hair, beautiful eyes, and handsome to look at." David's physical appearance alludes to the differing aspects of his personality. His ruddiness suggests a warlike nature, while his eyes and general appearance indicate kindness and gentility.[9]

At first Samuel doubted whether David could be the one worthy of the kingship, a forerunner of the dynasty that would lead the Jewish people to the end of time. He thought to himself, "This one will shed blood as did the red-headed Esau."[10]

God saw, however, that David's greatness was that he would direct his aggressiveness toward positive aims. God commanded Samuel, "My anointed one is standing before you, and you remain seated? Arise and anoint David without delay! For he is the one I have chosen!"[11]

As Samuel held the horn of oil, it bubbled, as if it could not wait to drop onto David's forehead. When Samuel anointed him, the oil hardened and glistened like pearls and precious stones, and the horn remained full.

As Samuel anointed David, the sound of weeping could be heard from outside the great hall. It was the voice of Nitzevet, David's lone supporter and solitary source of comfort.

Her twenty-eight long years of silence in the face of humiliation were finally coming to a close. At last, all would see that the lineage of her youngest son was pure, undefiled by any blemish. Finally, the anguish and humiliation that she and her son had borne would come to an end.

Facing her other sons, Nitzevet exclaimed, "The stone that was reviled by the builders[12] has now become the cornerstone!" (Psalms118:22)

Humbled, they responded, "This has come from God; it was hidden from our eyes" (ibid. verse 23).

Those in the hall cried out in unison, "Long live the king! Long live the king!" Within moments, the once-reviled shepherd boy became the anointed future king of Israel.

Nitzevet's Legacy

King David would have many more trials to face until he was acknowledged by the entire nation as the new monarch to replace King Saul. During his kingship, and throughout his life, up until his old age, King David faced many ordeals.

King David possessed many great talents and qualities which would assist him in attaining the tremendous achievements of his lifetime. Many of these positive qualities were inherited from his illustrious father, Yishai, after whom he is fondly and respectfully called *ben Yishai,* the son of Yishai.

But it was undoubtedly from his mother that the young David absorbed the fortitude and courage to face his adversaries. From the moment he was born, and during his most tender years, it was Nitzevet who, by example, taught him the essential lesson of valuing every individual's dignity and refraining from embarrassing another, regardless of the personal consequences. It was she who displayed a silent but stoic bravery and dignity in the face of the gravest hardship.

It is from Nitzevet that King David absorbed the strength, born from an inner confidence, to disregard the callous treatment of the world and find solace in the comfort of one's Maker. It was this strength that would fortify King David to defeat his staunchest antagonists and his most treacherous enemies, as he valiantly fought against the mightiest warriors on behalf of his people.

Nitzevet taught her young child to find strength in following the path of one's inner convictions, irrespective of the cruelty that might be hurled at him. Her display of patient confidence in the Creator that justice would be served gave David the inner peace and solace that he would need, over and over again, in confronting the formidable challenges in his life. Rather than succumb to his afflictions, rather than become the individual who was shunned by his tormentors, David learned from his mother to stand proud and dignified, feeling consolation in communicating with his Maker in the open pastures.

She demonstrated to him, as well, the necessity of boldness while pursuing the right path. When the situation would call for it, personal risks must be taken. Without her bold action in taking the place of her maidservant that fateful night, the great soul of her youngest child, David, the forebear of Moshiach, would never have descended to this world.

The soul-stirring psalms composed by King David in his greatest hours of need eloquently describe his suffering and heartache, as well as his faith and conviction. The book of Psalms gives a voice to each of us, and has become the balm to soothe all of our wounds, as we too encounter the many personal and communal hardships of life in *galut* (exile).

As we say these verses, our voices mesh with Nitzevet's, with King David's, and with all the voices of those past and present who have experienced unjustified pain, in beseeching our Maker for that time when the "son (descendant) of David" will usher in the era of redemption, and true justice will suffuse creation.

FOOTNOTES

1.

Translation taken from *The Living Nach*, published by Moznaim.

2.

Siftei Kohen, Vayeishev.

3.

See I Samuel17:34-36

4. The story and concepts in this chapter are based on *Yalkut HaMachiri*, as well as *Sefer HaTodaah* (section on Sivan and Shavuot). See also an interesting English rendition in the book *Don't Give Up*, pp. 187ff.

5.

See Genesis ch. 38, and Midrashim and commentaries on that chapter.

6.

In the verse in the psalm where David says he was a "stranger" to his brothers, the Hebrew word for stranger, *muzar*, is from the same root as *mamzer*—bastard, illegitimate offspring.

7.

Commentaries of Radak and Abarbanel to 1 Samuel16:3.

8.

A short while after this coronation feast, David was instructed by his father to visit Eliav at the battlefield. A war with the Philistines was imminent, and Eliav lashed out in anger at David. This tendency to anger disqualified Eliav now from the throne. (This event occurred after David was anointed as king. However, according to the commentaries, it is possible that they didn't understand the implications of the anointing, assuming that Samuel had designated David as a new student in his school of prophecy. Though this was an honor, and an act that would validate David's lineage, only once David actually became king over the entire nation did his brothers realize his true greatness.)

9.

Malbim.

10.

Bereishit Rabbah 63:8.

11.

Midrash Tanchuma, Va'eira 6.

12.

The Hebrew word in this verse for "builders," *bonim*, is the same root as the word for "sons.

Can I continue without saying about Jesus being God the creator of the creation? Not at all. Let deal with that in the following words.

3. Jesus is God of gods and Lord of lords.

One day I was discussing with a friend of mine who was a member of Jehovah witness. He was telling me that Jesus is not God the creator. He used some scriptures and I demonstrated that Jesus is the only true God the creator of the universe as described in the holy bible. When I showed him another scripture that proved him wrong, he said:" I am going to rethink about that."The devil knows that once we acknowledge Jesus as God and not as a mere prophet like Moses and Elijah, then we have won over him.

Jesus is the Jehovah but who came in the world with a human body in the name of Jesus. In the plan of God was to reveal himself to His created and teach them how to worship the true God, their maker. Before Jesus came, God used Moses, prophets as the mediator between a man and God. They were human beings and therefore they were imperfect vessels of God. There was a need of a perfect one who is God himself. And that was His majesty Jesus Christ the living True God.

Water that is pure and passes through an impure pipe becomes contaminated with some impurity. The water is no longer pure and it is not good for health.

Our heavenly father used to send human beings to teach his law like Moses and other prophet like the Prophet Elijah but they were like imperfect pipe, imperfect vessels. God had to come down himself in the name of Jesus Christ to teach us how to love him and worship in the proper manner.

Jesus was without sin because He is God. He was not from Adam. Jesus asked Pharisees:" **Can any of you prove me guilty of sin? If I am telling the truth, why don't you believe me?** *John 8:46, New International Version.*

You cannot remove a sin while yourself you have sins. So Jesus because He was God therefore He was the right one to come in the world and take away the sin of the world caused by the rebellion of Adam.

He is from heaven, from God himself. *In the book of* **Luke 1:35** *. We read:"The angel answered and said to her (Mary the mother of Jesus), "The Holy Spirit will come upon you and the power of the Most High will overshadow you; and for that reason the holy Child shall be called the* **Son of God***.*

It appears at **John 1:29***, where John the Baptist sees* **Jesus** *and exclaims, "Behold the* **Lamb of God** *who takes away the sin of the world."*

Jesus knew and defended that He was God. Jesus, in response to the Pharisees' question "Who do you think you are?" said, "'your father Abraham rejoiced at the thought of seeing my day; he saw it and was glad.' 'You are not yet fifty years old,' the Jews said to him, 'and you have seen Abraham!' 'I tell you the truth,' Jesus answered, 'before Abraham was born, I am!' At this, they picked up stones to stone him, but Jesus hid himself, slipping away from the temple grounds"

*(**John 8:56–59**). The violent response of the Jews to Jesus' "I AM" statement indicates they clearly understood what He was declaring—that He was the eternal God incarnate. Jesus was equating Himself with the "I AM" title God gave Himself in **Exodus 3:14**.*

*If Jesus had merely wanted to say He existed before Abraham's time, He would have said, "Before Abraham, I was." The Greek words translated "was," in the case of Abraham, and "am," in the case of Jesus, are quite different. The words chosen by the Spirit make it clear that Abraham was "brought into being," but Jesus existed eternally (see **John 1:1**).*

*There is no doubt that the Jews understood what He was saying because they took up stones to kill Him for making Himself equal with God (**John 5:18**). Such a statement, if not true, was blasphemy and the punishment prescribed by the Mosaic Law was death (**Leviticus 24:11–14**). But Jesus committed no blasphemy; He was and is God, the second Person of the Godhead, equal to the Father in every way.*

To the all my beloved and great people who are in Judaism and Islam, I would like to show again that the God of Jacob, the God of Abraham has been revealed to the World in the name of Jesus Christ.

*In the book of **Revelation 22:13** Jesus said to Apostle John:"I am the Alpha and the Omega, the first and the last, the beginning and the end."; we read also in **Revelation 1:8**:"I am the Alpha and the Omega," says the Lord God, "who is and who was and who is to come, the Almighty."; **Revelation 21:6** :"Then He said to me, "It is done I am the Alpha and the Omega, the beginning and the end I will give to the one who thirsts from the spring of the water of life without cost."*

*Let me also add the verses respectively **Revelation 1:17** and **Revelation 2:8** :"When I saw Him, I fell at His feet like a dead man And He placed His right hand on me, saying, "Do not be afraid; I am the first and the last, "And to the angel of the church in Smyrna write: The first and the last, who was dead, and has come to life, says this:"*

*In the old testament we find that Jesus is the same in old testament and the new testament when we read in the book of Isaiah where the God of Jacob called himself like the **First and the Last**:"*

***Isaiah 44:6**"Thus says the LORD, the King of Israel and his Redeemer, the LORD of hosts: 'I am the **first and I am the last**, and there is no God besides Me.*

Isaiah 48:12**"Listen to Me, O Jacob, even Israel whom I called; I am He, **I am the first, I am also the last.

***Isaiah 41:4**"Who has performed and accomplished it, Calling forth the generations from the beginning? 'I, the LORD, am **the first, and with the last I am He**.""*

These verses demonstrate that Jesus is the Same God in the Old Testament and in the New Testament.

*Jesus is given the name of **Lord of lords** in the New Testament which is also found in the Old Testament meaning that Jesus Christ is the same God in the Old Testament and in the New Testament:*

Proof in the New Testament

*In **Revelation 19:16** we read:"On his robe and on his thigh he has a name written, **King of kings** and **Lord of lords**." And we read also in **Revelation 17:14** They will make war on the*

*Lamb, and the Lamb will conquer them, for he is **Lord of lords** and **King of kings**, and those with him are called and chosen and faithful."*

Proof of the calling of God the Lord of lords from the Old Testament.

Deuteronomy 10:17:" *For the Lord your God is God of gods and Lord of lords, the great, the mighty, and the awesome God, who is not partial and takes no bribe.";*

Psalm 136:2-3: *"Give thanks to the **God** of **gods**. His love endures forever.*

*Give thanks to the **Lord of lords**,*

For his steadfast love endures forever;"

*This is the proof that our beloved Lord and Savior Jesus Christ is the same God in the Old Testament and the New Testament. He is the **God of gods**; the God of Abraham, Isaac and Jacob who created us and who deserves and he only **worship** forever and ever. There is no power, no king, and no lord who can oppose Him and win! Hallelujah! Halleluiah!*

Shame the devil by your worship while kneeling down

Satan always look the best that God always look for because he knows what that is the best God desires a lot that moves His heart.

When Satan was tempting he told Jesus:" If you bow down and worship me, I will give all the kingdoms of the earth!" But our always overcomer, our good friend Jesus Christ rebuked Satan and said:" It is written you shall worship God and serve Him only!"

This kind of worship is the best that the devil was looking from His Creator Jesus Christ for Satan to grant to Jesus the kingdoms of the world.

asking for Jesus to

I like to worship my Lord Jesus Christ and spend some times before the Lord kneeling down as a sacrifice of thanksgiving for having died for me and the whole world just to shame the devil.

One day I ask a certain pastor:" Here in Zambia you like to kneel down to show a respect to someone who deserve honor but how many times do you kneel down when you are praying God?"

It is no easy to kneel down; it is painful. Then I understood why to kneel down in worship to God is the best because it is a sacrifice in its own.

One night I was praying and took more than one hour praying kneeling down to shame the devil and I heard a voice saying like:" If you worship me and bow down before me, I will make everything bow down to you!" In order words God will make turn a "none" into a "yes". He will make disobedient people obedient by His power.

He will make what is impossible possible. He will make all rulers of the earth obey and serve me! God instructed princes through the prophet of God Ezechiel to bow down in worship while in temple! If you do not have your legs, you can still worship God in your heart because the true worshipper God is looking for is a person who worships God in true and in Spirit and that means worship out of your heart.

God is interested by a true worship from your heart expressed physically knelling down or lifting up your hands as a sign of surrender the own Moses used to overcome the enemy while Joshua was on the ground fighting against the enemy. Any revelation that worked in the past was also revealed to us in our time. But the Holy Spirit is the one who can lead you what kind of weapon you need to use in prayer for a particular situation.

My beloved people from all the world let's spend some times kneeling down in worship before the King of kings our Lord, and God Jesus Christ and give this kind of worship to Jesus for the glory of our heavenly Father and bring shame to the devil.

Chapter 2. The promises to King David, my own blessings!

"Therefore I tell you, whatever you ask in prayer, believe that you have received it, and it will be yours."

Jesus said in **Mark 11:24.**

When I was in my room praying a certain Saturday after dedicating myself to the Lord as King David in my time in the name of Jesus Christ; the Holy Spirit led me in the scripture in Isaiah55:3-5:

"Listen now, my people, and come to me; come to me, and you will have life! I will make a lasting covenant with you and give you the blessings I promised to David.

I made him a leader and commander of nations, and through him I showed them my power.

Now you will summon foreign nations; at one time they did not know you, but now they will come running to join you! I, the LORD your God, the holy God of Israel, will make all this happen; I will give you honor and glory." **Good News Translation** version.

When I saw these powerful promises I knew I have right to receive them through Christ who died for the Humanity. I am also a descendant of Abraham and David through Christ Jesus through his blood that His majesty our good Lord, God and friend shed for all humanity and forever.

And I prayed:*" Father, I receive those blessings promised to David to be a leader and a commander of nations."*

But how many nations? I know God is serious in all his promises. **He does not joke!**

I remembered what God told Abraham our Father through faith in Christ:"*for all the land that you see I will give to you and to your offspring forever*."Genesis 13:15, **English Standard Version.**

I understand that **God will give you what you see**. Then I said Father, the land I am seeing is the **Whole world**. But I doubt and asked myself if Christ Jesus my Lord and my God is willing to give as his king to rule the whole world. The bible says that to believe in God equals to please Him. **I like to please my dearest heavenly Father and God!**

Jesus died for the sins of all humanity. Through his death he gave birth to all people of all times. The land that Jesus is interested in is the whole World. We are all his seed, his descendants, his offspring, his children, his sons and daughters(**Isaiah 53:10**). God no longer interested in the only one nation of Israel. He died for the whole world for all generations. Moreover, In **Isaiah9:6**:" *For to us a Child is born, to us a Son is given; and the government shall be upon His shoulder, and His name shall be called Wonderful Counselor, Mighty God, Everlasting Father [of Eternity], Prince of Peace.*

We all know this son is Jesus When you are praying for the state of Israel you should pray also for Palestine and all Arabs nations because *Jesus , the God of Abraham is the God of all the earth, all nations*. Therefore start praying and thinking as a world citizen and pray for all nations instead of praying only for your small nation, tribe…

Remember, that as descendants of Christ we are the descendants of David, the descendants of Abraham by faith in our dearest Christ Jesus who cried because of the extreme suffering at the cross" *My God, my God why have you abandoned me*?

The God the Father knew his mission of making the whole World His people but not only the nation of Israel. God planned to create a **great new kingdom of Israel which is the Whole World, all the Earth.**

After wondering if to ask God to be the King, a ruler and commander of all nations is in the will of God, the Holy Spirit led to **Psalm89:27** Where Jehovah revealed to me a promise to King David in the name of Jesus Christ in our time:"

I will also make him my firstborn (preeminent), the highest of the kings of the earth" in order words, all the nations will serve him and all kings will bow down to Him.

God promised that He will give me the blessings promised to King David; therefore I receive to be the highest of all leaders of the Earth in Jesus 'name! I occupied a vacant place of someone who comes in the name of the almighty God, Jesus Christ!

If my beloved and great man **US president Donald Trump** can try to keep his words promised to my beloved great people of America during his campaign where it is possible, how more our God who is the almighty one can promise every word and fulfill it without any hindrance because nothing can resist to his WILL! Our dear mighty Lord and God Jesus Christ is in heaven but He wants his people to rule on the earth and bring the heavenly kingdom and the divine will on the earth!

My wonderful protector and Savior Jesus Christ is the one who promised King David those promise in his time and so did he in my time. Jesus Christ said in **JOHN 8:56-59**:" *Your father Abraham rejoiced to see My day, and he saw it and was glad.*" 57 Then the Jews said to Him,

"You are not yet fifty years old, and You have seen Abraham?" 58 Jesus said to them, "Truly, truly, I say to you, before Abraham was, I AM."

"**I AM**" is the name God gave Himself in **Exodus 3:13-14**: *"Then Moses said to God, "Indeed, when I come to the children of Israel and say to them, 'The God of your fathers has sent me to you,' and they say to me, 'What is His name?' what shall I say to them?" And God said to Moses, "I AM WHO I AM." And He said, "Thus you shall say to the children of Israel, 'I AM has sent me to you.'"* Jesus was declaring to them in terms that are crystal clear to them that He is God. Jesus Christ is called "Ancient of days" first appears in **Daniel 7:9**.

I understood that Jesus Christ is the same one who promised all the blessings to David and He always look for a man with whom He can work with to rule nations and establish the Kingdom of God on earth.

In the time of David He was interested only in a one holy nation of Israel. Israel was a pilot holy nation but heaven had a big plan for the whole world as a **WORLD HOLY NATION.**

God is interested in all nations and the devil; Satan is interested in all nations as well. Satan has tried to rule the world but in vain. It is time for the Holy people of God to do it for the glory of our God. The children of the devil are determined but the church must wake up and be more determined to take over. This is the season; this is the hour of the manifestation of the sons of God.

Another promise made to King David and his descendants is written in Psalm2:8-9:"**Ask Me, and I will make the nations Your inheritance, the ends of the earth Your possession.** *You*

will break them an iron scepter; You will shatter them like pottery." *In other words you will rule them with great power.*

Who are supposed to be shattered? The enemy of the Lord Jesus Christ. It is said in 1 **Samuel 2:10:"**

Those who oppose the LORD will be shattered. He will thunder from heaven against them. The LORD (here is about His majesty the king of kings and Lord of lords Jesus Christ) will judge the ends of the earth and will give power to His king. He will exalt the horn of His anointed."

Do you want to know a testimony proving how true the word of God it is?

I have come to fulfill this prophecy. It is not good at all to oppose God and His anointed King. Whatever God has done through His Word no one can oppose that unless you want destruction.

God is ready to shatter every opponent to His vision through me. Let me share with you a testimony:" ***Someone was disrespecting me and opposing my honor. The bible says those who deserve honor give them honor. I kept quiet but I prayed the same night:"Lord you have already made me your King and no one should disrespect me. So whoever disrespects me is disrespecting you. Therefore you said that you rebuke those you love. So, I do not want my friends continue with this behavior and because I love them Father plague with a sudden punishment just to make them respect your king and do what is right with God. And when you have done that make them understand that what will happen is because of their sin.***

The following day before lunch hour, something happened and a friend of mine reported that. I praised how faithful my God is and I saw how I will be working through His power to make

nations change their fake ways through the power of our heavenly father in the love I have for all nations. You rebuke those you love. That day those who tried to disrespect God and His anointed King (I am who I am because of His word. I did not appoint myself but the God Himself through HIS UNCHANGEABLEWORD did.)

My God corrected my beloved people and started honoring me. They lost some money because of their disobedience but when they started doing the righteousness of God I prayed to my God to give them more than what they lost. I punished as a father punishes his children with love toward them. I praise my God the Maker of all things, my Father and the Rock of my salvation for having showed me His power, I am so grateful for His favor and grace toward me in the name of Jesus Christ my redeemer. Later on, I prayed to God to give them more than what they lost. **God does command us to forgive but also to make righteous people**! The bible says that **love** and **faithfulness** go before our God.

A king who comes in the name of Jesus can win or saved with or without a great army (**Psalm33**) simply because the God of David is with Him. The armory of God is immense and more powerful than nuclear weapon. It is also written that *do not touch my anointed*!

Jesus Christ promised to give the following word to the believer as It is written in **Revelation 2:27**:"

He will rule them with an iron scepter and shatter them like pottery--just as I have received authority from My Father." Jesus is ruling as King of kings and apply justice.

It is written also in **Zechariah12:8** that *the descendants of David will lead the people like God (Jesus) himself, like an angel of God.*

I am a descendant of David by faith through Jesus Christ who is a descendant of David; therefore I will lead the world as God (Jesus) himself, as angel of God. I have too and Jesus himself will help His chosen ones from all over the world for the sake of His name!

Moreover the promises of **Isaiah11** are mine because through Christ Jesus I am also a righteous branch of Jesse:*"The Spirit of the Lord will rest on him— the Spirit of wisdom and of understanding, the Spirit of counsel and of might, the Spirit of the knowledge and fear of the Lord— [3] and he will delight in the fear of the Lord.*

He will not judge by what he sees with his eyes, or decide by what he hears with his ears; [4] but with righteousness he will judge the needy, with justice he will give decisions for the poor of the earth. He will strike the earth with the rod of his mouth; with the breath of his lips he will slay the wicked. [5] Righteousness will be his belt and faithfulness the sash around his waist."

I am a son of Abraham by faith through Christ and that is why all nations will be blessed through me!

I have right to receive the blessings adapted to my time made by King David to his son King Solomon in his time. King Solomon is no longer alive but I am the descendant of King David ready to in order of David in the name of Jesus Christ. And we are in the best time to fulfill the will of God through the blessings of God made to the descendants of King David a man of God who was a prophet of God. Those prayers of King David are found in **Psalm72:1-20** (New International Version):" Endow the king with your justice, O God, the royal son with your righteousness. May he judge your people in righteousness, your afflicted ones with justice.

May the mountains bring **prosperity** to the people, the hills the fruit of righteousness. **May he defend the afflicted among the people and save the children of the needy; may he crush the oppressor.**

May he endure[a] as long as the sun, as long as the moon, through all generations. May he be like rain falling on a mown field, like showers watering the earth. In his days may the righteous flourish and prosperity abound till the moon is no more.

May he rule from sea to sea and from the River[b] to the ends of the earth. May the desert tribes bow before him and his enemies lick the dust. May the kings of Tarshish(This can be adapted to our generation) and of distant shores

bring tribute to him.
May the kings of Sheba and Seba(This one also can be adapted to our generation) present him gifts.
May all kings bow down to him and all nations serve him.

For he will deliver the needy who cry out, the afflicted who have no one to help.
He will take pity on the weak and the needy and save the needy from death.
He will rescue them from oppression and violence, for precious is their blood in his sight.

Long may he live!
May gold from Sheba be given him!
May people ever pray for him and bless him all day long.
May grain abound throughout the land; on the tops of the hills may it sway.
May the crops flourish like Lebanon and thrive[c] like the grass of the field.
May his name endure forever; may it continue as long as the sun.

Then all nations will be blessed through him, [d]
and they will call him blessed.

Praise be to the Lord God, the God of Israel,
who alone does marvelous deeds.
Praise be to his glorious name forever;
may the whole earth be filled with his glory.

Amen and Amen.

This concludes the prayers of David son of Jesse.

Footnotes:

a. **Psalm 72:5** Septuagint; Hebrew *You will be feared*

b. **Psalm 72:8** That is, the Euphrates

c. **Psalm 72:16** Probable reading of the original Hebrew text; Masoretic Text *Lebanon, / from the city*

d. **Psalm 72:17** Or *will use his name in blessings* (see Gen. 48:20)

Chapter 3. Promises of David in action in me.

After I gave myself to my beloved Christ Jesus who accepted to be slaughtered for the sin of the world, I started seeing miracles, the power or the glory of God in my life. According to **Isaiah**

55:4. "I made him a leader and commander of nations, and through him I showed them my power."**Good News Translation**.

1. Miraculous healing of my mother with her cancer.

 One day someone, a church mate to my mother told her that he heard a voice:'' Tell Bernadette that I am about to take her home".

Some days later she was diagnosed with liver cancer with advanced cirrhosis. She was 60 years old. A God fearing- woman who liked to make people laugh. Bernadette my late mother was a lover of people.

When she showed me the medical test result that proved the diagnosis, it was no easy for me to accept it. I hid from her letting know of that fatal condition. I loved her so much and I did not to disturb her peace with the diagnosis.

I remembered what she told me how she fought painfully and patiently during the labor for my birth. There was no medication to cure her and I knew what was going to happen for her. I did not want her to pass away before I graduate. I wanted her to be around at my degree cerebration. She encouraged me, she gave me whatever she could give me; sometimes she would give me her money she had saved maybe for something else.

Looking at what my father and late mother offered to me I can see why our papa God commanded us to honor a father and a mother. Therefore they deserve a pure honor from the children. Honor could mean the time we have to put aside for our beloved parents no matter how busy we are and listen to them speaking. Laugh with them, Give them a gift whether they are rich or not.

A gift from your beloved one especially your relatives as children mean always something great. If you put your parents somewhere alone to be taken care by other people who are not their relatives because they are too old to be kept by you and leave them in the old people homes when they as a baby they did not abandoned to yourself, I do not think it is fair at all! Never see them as a burden but a source of your blessing. I read from somewhere that a burden means is " employment, occupation or responsibility."

Government should help children via some just laws to honor their parents for the good of those children and the nation. The bible tells us that it is not the *hardworking that make one rich or wealthy but the blessing of the Lord God! If you are not blessed by your parents your hardworking may not make you happy and richer as wished. Even your blessings may be cursed.*

When you take care of your parents with all your heart and love them as someone who loves God because God is hidden in them, you are only attracting blessings:

" I remember when my mother was sick in her last days I used to spend time with her though she was in coma. I did not have enough time because I had to write an exam and it was my last chance in the last year of my medical study, the seventh year of medicine.

I had written the same exam when I had more than enough time but I failed. My mother was sick, I was always busy praying for her and I had an exam that I had to write and succeed but that time I did not have enough time. Someone told me:" Your mother is dying but you are still alive, go home and prepare your exam!" But there is something that was in my mind: I did not want to abandon my mother. I would think what can be done for my beloved late mother to recover.

My mother used to tell me whenever I wronged her while a child, how painful was my birth time for her. She did not abandon me due to the pain but she accepted to undergo the hard process for me to see the beautiful creation of our God. So when she was dying I wanted to be nearby and escort her in peace.

I would check whatever I could do to make her less painful. Sometime I would propose doctors what to do. I wanted to stay with her till the last day.

Sometimes I would advise even my professor who was treating her at a private hospital. My question was:"what can be done for my mother to recover?" I was following her health carefully.

In the night I would go home and prepare my exam. Guess what? I succeeded that exam with good marks without possessing enough time to prepare while I did not manage to succeed when I had enough time to prepare the same exam. I wrote the exam few days after her death.

There is blessing in taking care of our beloved parents physically or in prayer when you are not near them. Spend time with them thinking about them and letting them know that you love them. You will never go wrong in doing that to your parents. If there is anything wrong you may think they did to you; just love them and forgive them because what they gave you cannot be bought anywhere else. They deserve your unconditional attention and love.

I could not believe that the cancer could be healed. Then I prayed: *" Lord God you told me that you will show your power to nations through me, if you heal my mother's cancer completely and if even if you are determined to take her home please show me your power and let her die with another disease but not cancer then I will know that the promises to David are mine also and I will tell nations how you healed the cancer miraculously."*

I said to my heavenly Father:'' I am going to use this medicine which was like a just a painkiller as a medicine to cure her cancer in the name of Jesus Christ! David to kill Goliath he used a stone and a sling, as a medical doctor a stone was that medicine in the name of the Lord Jesus Christ!"

The cancer that was diagnosed by two of my lecturers at University was completely healed without any trace of cancer according to my prayer through the name of the Savior of the whole World His majesty Jesus Christ who is the King of kings and Lord of lords.

"How can you explain there is no more of cancer in Bernadette my mother?"I asked my experienced lecturer who worked for many years in South Africa.

"I don't know". He replied to me.

But When I saw she healed completely with her cancer I said:" *Thank you so much my God to heal that cancer, you have shown me your power through your name and if you are willing you can also heal her cirrhosis but let it be according to your will. If you want to take her home do it and I know that all things work together for our good according to the purpose you have for our life and the plans you have for your righteous people are for good and not for harm.*"

I prayed like that because God allows some circumstances to happen for our good depending to where we are going. Jesus for instance had to pass through suffering to save the World of their sins hence He prayed:" Father if you are willing let this cup pass me but let your will be done and not mine!" But where you know it is a promise from God then you are sure you are praying in the will of God, therefore be sure that you have already received what you are asking for in prayer according what our beloved Lord and God Jesus Christ said in Mark11.24

"Mum, the Lord has healed you the cancer you had and that I disclose it to you and if he want to heal you completely He can do that." Finally I confessed to my beloved late mother about her condition.

She died in 2014 due to cirrhosis and I said the public during her burial that even if my mother passed on I was happy because the Lord has given me my heart's desire which was "my mother not to die due to her liver cancer."

The God of David is a God of miracles and since that day the Lord proved me that he has chosen me to be called "David" and has given me all the promises he gave to David. The fear of cancer despaired within me. Jesus said you cannot receive them unless it has been given to you." In other words, when we receive a spiritual word, God is behind your welcoming the word in you: Its plantation, watering and growth according to His purpose through us His beloved children.

The God of David is alive and the bible says:" Jesus is the same yesterday, today, tomorrow and forever more" why? Of course because He is God of gods and Lord of lords.

It is also written that "nothing is impossible with God" of course when God is willing and "**If God is with you who can be against with you?**"

I love and praise you dear heavenly Father for choosing me and show your power to nations through me and for giving me the garment of your beloved David in this last days through the mighty name of the Lord of all nations forevermore Jesus Christ who died for the sin of humanity! Thank you!

2. Saved when I cried out:"Save your king oh God!"

 In 2016, I decided to leave the country of Burundi that I love so much where I was born through a great womb of my great late mother. I did know where exactly to go but I have to leave because of the political trouble that was happening there due to a president Peter NKURUNZIZA (a great man I love when he is praising God and who submitted the nation of Burundi to the Lord Almighty Jesus Christ along with the great first lady Denise Nkurunziza his lovely wife.) who stood for the third term against the constitution according to his opponents.

I am the first born in a family of three(3) sons and one beautiful sister. Before the political trouble our second born was already gone in South Africa because of fear that was in every Burundian, a small but great country that was colonized first by my beloved and great people of Germany and later my great and beloved people of Belgium was privileged to touch with their feet the Burundian soil as colonialist. Belgium colonized Burundi and Rwanda and considered Rwanda and Burundi as one great nation hence they used to call them "Ruanda-Urundi with Bujumbura their capital". These two nations Burundi and Rwanda are like Twins because both of them have almost the same local language and the same 3 components of the population: the great people of Hutu, the great people of Tutsi and the third one are the great people of Twa.

"If it was not your bible you are holding in your hands, you were going to be considered as one of the trouble makers that demonstrated against the president Peter Nkurunziza! " That was what a policeman told our third born when he was visiting a family Hutu that we love who was living in a province called Rumonge.

After my beloved brother was saved because he was carrying a bible in his hands, my brother, our second born sent for him to join him in South Africa. I remember what I told him" **you should love the holy Bible all your life."**

Our parents never taught us to think only as Tutsi but we were raised as children born everybody as our brothers and sisters without considering their race, tribe, nation, color of the skin...etc.

My late beloved mother used to say that our "differences on our dear planet are like flowers on a mountain and so we should love each other without any problem.

I was raised in the same way the parents(May their souls rest in peace!) of a great man I love, the former US president George W. Bush was raised from when they taught him to love everybody including black people. I liked something George W. Bush wrote in his book that he refused to consider himself in one "box ".

I remained in Burundi with my beloved wonderful father and my dearest and intelligent sister our last born who is very loved by our great Daddy. But later on she left for Kenya one of nations including Burundi of the great East Africa Community.

Most young medical doctors like me went to work in Rwanda, Kenya...I had a promise to in charge of a clinic belonging to a good man who was advisor to his excellence the president Peter Nkurunziza but I had already decided to leave the country.

Do you want to know what fueled my leaving decision? On 11 December 2015, many young people were killed because some people who were against the president went in different Burundian military camps in Bujumbura, the capital city of Burundi to attack them. It was if I do not forget the military camp of Ngagara and ISCAM (Institut supérieur des cadres militaries in French or Higher Institute of Military Staff in English) and other military camps.

After their defeat; the government looked for them up to their different area of residents according to some news. One of those areas was Jabe where I was staying in the house of my great beloved Aunt with her husband, a great man I love with a good and wonderful character. The time of that battle my Aunt was already staying in the country of the great people of Germany.

Early in the morning I woke up hearing the sound of guns near our home where I was alone with my beloved cousins. The great man, the husband of my Aunt was not at home because he was in mission work for the national Radio and television of Burundi (RTNB).

"My God! Protect your king the same way you protected the Israelites in Goshen in the country of Egypt(When God was punishing Egypt for them to release the people of Israel, the Lord God made sure that nothing bad that was touching Egypt would touch Israel)!" I cried to my beloved heavenly Father in prayer that fearful morning surrounded by guns sound shot

Immediately After cry to my God, the Holy Spirit deposited a song in my heart that assured me of God's protection. God is spirit and He speaks to our spirit. The same way God you can touch your spirit even God you cannot touch Him but Him He touches us and He knows everything about us. I am very grateful to God for giving me such wonderful wisdom! I love my heavenly Father! The song was not brought in my spirit by my biological father or uncle but my God, the creator of all flesh. I like to trust in God and then have peace like a baby on the hands of a mother.

All of the sudden, an extraordinary peace took place in me and I took my breakfast.

Guess what happened? The houses of Our 2 neighbors were shot but us who were in the middle of our two neighbors nothing touched us! People died in other avenue but not anyone died along our avenue. The Lord protected our house. The God of the Bible is forever alive! That is a proof that whatever happened in the time of Moses can happen today because Jesus is the same today, yesterday , tomorrow and forever.

I praised Him because he heard our cry and helped us! It is written in **Jeremiah 17:7** that "**But blessed is the one who trusts in the LORD, whose confidence is in him.**" **New International Version**; and " **Cursed are those who put their trust in mere humans, who rely on human strength and turn their hearts away from the LORD.** "**Jeremiah 17:5, New Living Translation**. God is good! And it is also written that "**call upon the name of the Lord Jesus Christ and you will be saved!**"

Try to see the Bible as a book of Now and not only a book of history because His Word is alive forever! Whatever the Lord did in the past He is able to perform it today and even greater works according to the promise of our beloved God and Lord Jesus Christ the King of kings of all the earth!

After that I decided to leave Burundi toward my beloved and great people of Zambia with a testimony in my hand that the Lord Jesus Christ has saved His King by His powerful hand! Praise to Him for the glory of our great and almighty heavenly Father!

It is written about David how He was instructed to pray. **"He will cry to Me, 'You are my Father, My God, and the rock of my salvation." Psalm 89:26, New American Standard Bible.** That day I saw my God as the rock of my salvation.

3. To change a rule that was against my right at University: The spirit of David took over me.

When at primary and secondary school I used to be the first of my class; at university I did three (3) times the third year as a medical doctor. I am a man who would make by the grace of God my teachers proud of me and sometimes surprises them as an unknown intelligent guy.

One day at my secondary school called "Lycée du lack Tanganyika in French or lake Tanganyika high school " a teacher-from my beloved and great people of Democratic Republic of Congo(DRC) -who taught us mathematics was shocked when he was told that it was me the first of our class at the end of the first semester. Why? Because he was not expecting me to be so. I was not a guy who was often seen on the black board in the class or answering some questions. But when it came to write exam I would get the best marks.

During class, I was usually quiet, encouraging other to behave as good people, like to read books about good great men like Martin Luther King Junior, George W Bush and women (I like to read autobiography); enjoying making other people happy and laugh like my mother and father who; when I am with him he wants to greet almost every person he meets.

"Do you know what a ghost is?" My dear teacher of mathematics asked the class and explained that a ghost is something which is not seen by our physical eyes but it is there and busy working. He said this man is like a ghost. The class started calling me like so.

Now at university I was redoing my third year and the second year of medicine. It was hard for me to accept redoing a year because I was not used to. While I was still in the second year time of the same third year of medicine, my beloved cousin who was in England sent me something just to encourage me.

"What was that?' Oh he told me about **Dr Ben Carson**, a man I like from United State of America, a man that God used supernaturally during his career in the throughout the world as a neurosurgeon to be a great solution to the difficult situations that seemed impossible but when he prayed God would guide him and gave him victory.

 I remember asking my dear heavenly Father to use me to be a solution to different difficult cases in my medical career as well.

The God of Dr Ben is also my God and he can work miracles in my medical career through me by faith in Him because **"with God all things are possible**!" Praise to our wonderful and almighty heavenly Father in the mighty name of Jesus Christ!

When I succeeded my medical third year on the third time, I heard a voice in me declaring:" You will no longer redo any year until you finish your medical studies".

 God does speak because God who created our mouths to speak and our eyes and ears is surely expert in speaking, hearing and seeing. But you have to know that even the devil speaks also so you have to know how to distinguish the voice of God from to the one of the devil. The devil will always say something to confuse you and even use the scripture like what he did to our dearest Lord Jesus Christ. Sometimes he will use your nearest friends to make you lose focus toward your godly vision or mission like Peter to Jesus. Sometimes the devil would like to seduce and distract you by giving something interesting but against of your calling; That is why the devil may use the people to make you king because they have seen your kingship character while it is not your time and season. It happened to Jesus. Or some will try to make you what they are because they see some character like theirs, yet it is not your time and season. It is a battle to remain focused. Sometimes the devil may use prophets, parents, and brothers like what happened to David when he was a trying to know what was promised to a man who would kill Goliath.

Sometimes the devil may send you trials just to destroy your focus like apostle peter facing storm in the sea before he reaches his goal: To be where Jesus was. One should be careful and always remember who he is and who has sent him. You may be with for a longtime with chickens yet you are an eagle but that is not the reason to behave and think like chickens. Fight from your mind to remain who you are when focus changers are hitting badly.

Humility is not to be like what a man wants you to be but true humility is to be what God wants you to be.

Do not look for pleasing a man but only God but in all kindness. Remember if you want to go higher than your friends you have to separate yourself from them otherwise they will never let you go. Abraham had to leave his beloved family and country. He had to separate himself from his nephew Lot for him to hear God properly. If you separate yourself from your friends or relatives for a while does not mean hatred toward them. God had to use His power and push

Pharaoh to let Israel go. **To pursue your godly dream you have to wage war spiritually and physically but always putting on the armor of God like righteousness of God! King Solomon said it best: "Above all else, guard your heart, for it is the wellspring of life"** **(Proverbs 4:23).**

You people[le scientist like me, you people who do not want to believe there is no God, how do you call that voice that tell you an accurate information or guidance with you? Be wise and acknowledge your creator who is not seen physically by yourself but busy working. That voice is not from your uncle, your husband, your mother or father … but it is from God. You are a spirit and your creator is Spirit and when speaks he communicates directly with your spirit! Thank and praise your God for all his wise guidance he is giving you. The word of God said **Isaiah 30:21**

"You will hear a voice behind you saying, "This is the way. Follow it, whether it turns to the right or to the left." **GOD'S WORD Translation.**

Stop ignoring your God and his righteous laws because whether you like or not it will not benefit you but you are causing your own destruction. You do not worship our Lord Jesus as God himself and want to consider him as a simple prophet; you are destroying your own life!

Be wise because you will not win the battle therefore give him the honor He deserves as God. Read yourself the bible and ask God to reveal himself to you and stop believing and follow the mass. Your religion will not save you!

When my dear great man Trump became the US president his enemies were demonstrating against what God had already done in America. Some said:" He is not our president!" I laughed at them because whether you like it or not he was already the new US president.

When Jesus was physically among his creatures some did not to acknowledge him as a Son of God but to those who trusted in him He saved their life, He fed them, He healed them , He forgave their sin because He is God while others were not forgiven because they were busy saying He is making himself God . He refused to acknowledge him as the Messiah. Some they chose a destructive way of fighting him and become antichrist! Jesus Christ is the messiah, the Savior of the Humanity forever, **the Wonderful counselor, the Mighty God, the Eternal Father and the Prince of peace. Isaiah 9:6–7.**

The scripture is true forever. Who are you to use your small created brain to understand your creator? Between you and the pen you are using who is the greater? Who can manipulate another one, your pen or yourself? You can understand what you created and what you have in your hands but not the opposite. That is why it is written "**Trust in the Lord with all your heart and do not use your own understanding!" Proverbs 3:5.**

Your creator has power to manipulate you, to destroy you or to build you according to his will. He designed Solomon to be the next King after his father David but the brother to Solomon was busy fighting the will of God in vain because what our supreme Heavenly Father has decided no one can reverse! Our God is terrible ready to save when we call upon him or ready to destroy when somebody is busy fighting his plan!

He rejected King Saul and chose David as his king and shepherd to rule his people of Israel in his name but King Saul tried to fight the chosen king David. You know what? Whenever someone is trying to fight his plan God laughs! It is like the pen you are holding in your hands is trying to be against what you want to use it for, if you can laugh and says:" How come you can fight me and win when I have you in my hands? It is pure foolishness that is why what you can do it is only to laugh.

After Jesus rose from the death he is no longer working like a lamb but He is working like a lion, a king of kings and Lord of lords and the God of gods through those who believe Him! He is busy judging full of righteousness and justice of God not of a man.

He said: **"All authority in heaven and on earth has been given to me."**, Matthew 28Matthew28:18. Only God can say like that. Jesus Christ is going to rule the whole World using me. The time has come for Jesus to be worshiped as God all over the world and no one can resist for it is written, *As I live, saith the Lord, every knee shall bow to me, and every tongue shall confess to God.* **Romans 14:11 KJV**.

It is sad when people they do not give you the honor you deserve and they are busy trying to pull you down and fighting the God who gave you the honor and glory or they are trying to ignore you like what they do in not acknowledging that our wonderful and beloved Jesus Christ is God.

I know what it is when people they do not acknowledge who you are and whether they acknowledge your function, your role, they cannot change you but they are causing their own destruction because for you to be with them you are like a solution that God has sent to them. It happens somewhere in a certain family with whom I was staying instead of calling me when they have a medical condition in the family they would not call me but would avoid me and try to hide me from telling me what is going on. The person had an accident. I told the family that there is no need of CT SCAN but they did not believe me. They did the scan and the scan was of course normal but they have misused their money.

Another day I saw in a dream that the same person who had an accident from that same family was hospitalized and medically treated by a certain lady. I prayed against that dream fighting for the person who was a very friend of mine, a courageous man I love.

Some days later a member of that family got sick and was   handled medically by the same lady a sister in Christ I saw in the dream.

The patient had hypoglycemia and that happened when I was at the hospital and there was another doctor but the lady who was not a medical doctor did not ask me an advice though I was at the clinic. Yet the Lord helped me to resuscitate a patient with the same condition who was dying in other hospital when other health worker my colleagues had already announced the death of my patient from the other hospital.

The member of the family died and got the cause of the death from another colleague of mine who was a medical doctor himself at least consulted when it was already late. They preferred to use a person who is not a medical doctor while I was nearby. Hope the blood of that person is not on them!

They chose to ignore me; they lost humility while playing around a life of a person. I always remember what a teacher at university from Benin told us:" In medicine when you do not know you affirm that you do not know!" It is not only in medicine but in life generally humility is key for your success because you never know who hold in the hands the solution you need for your problem. And humility is not mediocrity but it is to ask advice from your colleagues or the people that has gone ahead of you. And it is important to listen to the voice that guides you to where you go for advice but not your mind.

You are a black; God may put the solution to your problem in the heart of a white person, so if you despise white people due to your stereotypes for example you may miss up your solution. The same if you are a white person God may put the solution in the heart of a black person, so if you despise white people due to your stereotypes for example you may miss up your solution. **Stereotypes kill you! Therefore love one another and respect one another!**

 I started confessing that I will no longer redo any year again repeating the voice I heard. I passed without problem the fourth year but I met a challenge during my fifth year.

Which challenge? You may ask.

I and other some of my classmates were told we cannot pass for the next year which was the sixth year, the first year of our internship before the seventh year the last of our medical studies as a general practitioner.

We were told that the jury has changed a rule which was not written as known in our academic rule. That rule was to tell us that we have to redo the fifth year. All my classmates to whom the new rule was going to affect their progress accepted the new rule. They did not choose to fight back before that challenge.

Sometimes there is a fake humility that you allow in your life and then cause your death! You have to fight back because there is something you can do against the difficulty with God's help unless the will of God is not there. It is important to pray to God before your abandon or resign. The challenge may be a way to your glory. And it may be the only opportunity in your life if you accept to fight. So do not give up to the enemy who is a stealer, destroyer, a killer of your progress, your destiny. Fight back!

And I said to myself:" If it was David was he going to accept people hindering him from progress because a human being has issued a declaration that was against a divine declaration?

"I will not redo this year in the name of Jesus Christ!" I fought against that hindrance through a fight of faith in the name of my God Jesus Christ; blessing my beloved teachers through a letter addressed to them. I knew that **if you bless someone it is not easy to receive back a curse but what it is easier is to receive back a blessing**. The bible says that David was wise in speaking. The bible says also that our mighty God and everlasting Father Jesus Christ, the creator of heavens and the earth judges and wages war in righteousness. (**Revelation19:11**)

I could confess -to myself and to whoever asked me if I had passed or not- that I had succeeded and that I was going to do my internship in pediatric department.

"They have vowed that no one with a note under 10 per 20 in pediatric course will not move to the next year!" Someone disclosed what the jury had decided against us. The vow is one but the vow to prevail is another thing. They had vowed and I had vowed in the name of Jesus that I would not redo the year. Who was going to win? The one backed by heaven was. God told David in Psalm89:24 that "*And in my name* — That is, by my favor and help-; *shall his horn be exalted* — He shall have both power and victory."

"The jury is sovereign", my dear lecturer of pediatric course mentioned that to me in the presence of the vice dean. She was a great woman and she taught us pediatric course very well.

When She said that Jury is sovereign; Immediately, I heard the Holy Spirit reminding me that my God is the sovereign God meaning He can change anything according to his will and for his glory that a human being has stated. **God has power to overrule**. That is why it is good to treat the people in need around you and not exploit their weakness because if they cry to God they can be answered against you who are mistreating them.

The Holy Spirit strengthened my faith and I was more determined to continue fighting for my right in the name of Jesus. I did the same thing King David did in **1 Samuel 30:6:" David was greatly distressed because the men were talking of stoning him; each one was bitter in spirit because of his sons and daughters**. But **David found strength in the LORD his God."**

"If you want you can go to the ministry of education for your case but we cannot change what we have decided here." The vice dean of the faculty of medicine told us.

A friend of mine told me also that they have permission from the government to update some rules but that information did not discourage me and moved me away from my faith in the Lord of lords the God of gods Jesus Christ.

"This thing will be corrected here in the name of Jesus Christ!" I declared to myself and to my friends who were advising me to go to the ministry of education for my case. The Lord Jesus Christ removed the fear of a man in me and only prevailed in me the voice of God.

Later on we met the dean of the faculty who told us that he is going to set up another commission for our case.

"You are admitted to the next year according to the former rule that allowed you to advance." A letter from the dean faculty was given to us with a positive answer to my request. God is faithful and "He is not a man that he can lie."

What is impossible with God? Nothing. I learnt that God is able to remove any obstacle and hindrance on your way toward your move. In the time of Jesus God killed King Herod who was against Jesus Christ! When you are with God no one can hinder you. God told Joshua:" **No one will be able to stand against you all the days of your life. As I was with Moses, so I will be with you; I will never leave you nor forsake you. Joshua 1:5.** That time I fought like David against my lecturers using the unfailing wisdom of God.

That new rule was removed for everyone who followed! I praise my dear heavenly Father for helping me and for giving me a nice victory like that. Thank you so much Jesus Christ for teaching me how to fight a good fight of faith and win through your name and in a righteous way! **I love you Jesus, my shield, my stronghold, my mentor and my almighty God forevermore!** Truly nations shall fear you lord Jesus and worship you as God according to your Word!

It is amazing how God can allow us to pass through some situations and make a way not only for yourself but for other people in your generation or the next generations to come.

4. The challenge to resuscitate a dying baby

After I graduate I was called to replace an American medical doctor at Kibuye hospital in the province of Gitega of my beloved and great nation of Burundi. The province is where my beloved late mother was born.

It was a hospital where many doctors from United State of America were helping to treat the Burundian people as missionaries. My job was to take care of the pediatric service and train medical students in the fifth and sixth year. I like teaching and I was happy when I was given the job by the medical director of the hospital who is a good and wise friend of mine full of the Holy Spirit of God, Dr Wilson Bizimana.

"Where is the pediatric doctor?" A certain competent nurse came right in my office where I was holding a meeting with my students in the morning before a round.

"Here I am. What's up?" I questioned him.

"There is a dying baby in the intensive care unit; we have tried but in vain." He replied.

I told him to look for another doctor obstetrician because I was quite busy with my students to whom I was giving some teachings the job I liked a lot but no one else was to be found around at the moment.

Finally I agree to go with them. They have already announced to parents of the baby to be ready for a burial. The baby was a handsome baby boy new born. I used my stethoscope and found the heart was still beating but very slowly. The hate rate was almost null. The whole body was not moving at all. I knew that those nurses in the reanimation room are well trained and if they come to look for a help it means that they have tried but in vain and there is no hope .

In front of that handsome but dying baby, I prayed to God in my heart to guide me for what to do and bring back to life the baby without any neurological complication because a brain without oxygen for sometimes (and that was after more than 30 minutes) becomes damaged.

And Immediately I heard a voice in me telling me to use glucose intravenous injection. I did not have time for biological examinations. I acted on the word and instructed my 2 intelligent and competent students with whom I was working. Immediately after the injection, the baby stretched out her hands and legs. The respiratory movements that were not there before were at the same time restored and the baby started breathing normally! I administered also aminophylline to prevent respiratory apnea and antbiotherapy to prevent an infection.

 The parents were very happy. I put the baby under observation and admitted the baby to continue the treatment. I did neurological examination which was positive. I asked her mother if the baby is breastfeeding normally. The answer was yes.

One day something strange happened!

I looked to the mother of the baby during a round some days later and said:" Make sure you raise your baby in the Word of God!"

"Okay doctor." The mother agreed with me, calmly. I was doing a round as usually in pediatric ward where I was working as a doctor in charge of the pediatric service.

Almost at the end of the round, I asked my students:"where is the baby that was dying before he came back to life."

"Doctor, the baby you are talking about is the one whose mother you instructed to "make sure she raises her baby in the Word of God." My students reminded me because them were every day with the patient admitted and would bring to me a difficult case because there were a lot of patients.

When they told me that I realized that what I told the mother of that baby was dictated by the Holy Spirit through me. I understood that God healed the baby for a reason that himself he can know. You are not a mistake you were born and survived a lot of calamities for a reason. You are not an accident. God protected you for a reason.

God told his prophet Jeremiah: **"Before I formed you in the womb I knew you, before you were born I set you apart; I appointed you as a prophet to the nations."** **Jeremiah 1Jeremiah1:5**. Therefore watch out the way you take care of your body, your life. You may have a problem with your creator the one who created your parents who gave birth to you if you behave carelessly and neglect yourself. You do not belong to yourself.

I thank God for using my hands to save the baby and I learnt a lesson. There are some situations that present themselves for you and only you to be a solution. You refuse to do something about that then you are rejecting your own responsibility. Do not look for others because those opportunities asking you to spend some time with people, family, to help some people with your hardly earned money have come to you not to harm or ruin you but to bless you, to make you happy, to multiply your life.

It is written that "It is the Lord's blessing that makes you wealthy. Hard work can make you no richer. **Proverbs 10:22**." How? Through your giving to support those in need! For example the fatherless, widow, foreigner, etc. You never lose anything when you are supporting others! The word of God is true forever.

It is said about David:" Then the Spirit came upon Amasai, the leader of the Thirty, and he said, "We are yours, David! We are on your side, son of Jesse. Peace and prosperity be with you, and **success to all who help you**, for your God is the one who helps you." So David let them join him, and he made them officers over his troops. " 1 **Chronicles 12:18, New Living Translation** .You see? Those who were going to help David for his ministry of ruling the people God was going to blessed their life.

As a scientist I like to act on the Word of God to experience the faithfulness of God because the bible says that God our Father is faithful. If you want to know God really do not just refuse the truth because you were taught the lies about Jesus because you may perish. Read the bible and try to find out the truth for yourself and ask Jesus Christ to reveal himself to you because He is not an idol but He is the only True God who created your mouth and ears; therefore He can hear you and answer you.

After I entered in a covenant with the God of gods Jesus Christ to use me like David in my time; I said" **Lord if you have really given me all the promises of David according to your promises, then Let me see that those who help me will get success and be blessed in what they do."**

What did I experience? In Zambia there was a man who whenever he was helping me; he would get blessed back immediately.

He told me one day:" Remember in your kingdom." I had told him how I was called David and the covenant between my God the Father and me.

Another lady gave me some money I needed and immediately she received more than what she gave me to help me for a particular need. Another person lost her phone after refusing to help me with that for a while. Jesus helped Peter to catch fishes after Peter helped Jesus to preach the gospel using the boat of Peter. When you support a work of God you are helping yourself.

You know what? The Word of God is not" **a placebo but a true and lasting medicine.**" The Word of our God who rose our Lord and Savior Jesus Christ the beloved of you Africa, Europe, south and North, Asia, Oceania, and all Islands.

God can send someone from a far to stay with you knowing that whatever the person needs for his mission and dream you are able to provide; but sometimes we avoid our responsibilities and therefore God look for another vessel to take care of his man because the ways of the Lord are more than one thousands! This is what the LORD says: "**Cursed is the one who trusts in man, who draws strength from mere flesh and whose heart turns away from the LORD. Jeremiah 17:5. New international Version.** Let me tell you when you help one in need with respect, cheerfully you gain a lot: happiness, success, long life, spiritual strength and righteousness of God that is spiritual prosperity. You get financial breakthrough as well.

You may say Dr David, Do you have any experience in your life of how this thing you are telling us is truth? Of course yes it is.

I was still a medical student and in the town of Bujumbura, I met a man about 45 years old, the face dark like me from Cameroun in the West Africa. A country that was colonized by France and England.

He told me about his name and we got to know each other. I like to see every human being as my own people, brothers and sisters because the God is one who made men and women with different colors of the skin and giving them different gifts according to his will. And then He gave his creation laws to govern them for their good. We have one source of our life that is why is called the Father of all us. It is written in **Isaiah 64Isaiah64:8" Yet you, Lord, are our Father.**

We   are   the   clay,   you   are   the   potter." Do you see why we should people from all over the World love each other and make sure that everyone on the earth is living well? We need each other; our Heavenly Father gave different natural resources in different regions of the World.

I think the reason why GOD said you shall not murder it is for the good of his people.

One day Jesus was hungry. And went to look for what to eat from a fig tree and found nothing. "He said to it, "May no one ever eat fruit from you again!" And His disciples were listening. **Mark 11:14, New American Standard Bible** ! Jesus cursed it. Jesus did not die with hunger God had to find another way for him but the fig tree that was born to be a solution for Jesus at that moment was cursed and destroyed.

The fig tree is like someone who was supposed to be a blessing to his neighbor but try to find some excuse not to help. And you say:" May God help you!" when it was you that God was ordained to use to help the person. Sometimes fear or worry, can hinder us from being a solution to the guy and then cause a curse for yourself and cause your own downfall. Be careful the way you handle some situations coming in your way to do something like to help whether using your resources, your skill or knowledge and so on or even to risk your life. But remember that **"where there is a high risk for a good cause there is a high of glory!"**

I said:"Oh Lord! Help my brother from Cameroun using my hand. I started supporting my brother from Cameroun with a 10 to 15 % of the money I was receiving from the government as bursary. I really appreciate all the governments from the former president Peter Buyoya who ruled the country of my beloved and great people of Burundi to Nkurunziza Peter the current president of Burundi now in 2019 for the support they did to me and to all the children of Burundi. I thank and praise God for them.

To cut short the story, I tried to look for my friend so called foreigner a job in the construction field because he was used to work in that field. I wanted to get something that he will do with pleasure. I know it is good to get a job doing what you like.

We got a job for him and he started getting good salary. He would invite me in a nice restaurant to share a meal with him. He was very happy. Please try to make happy the people around that you are treating like foreigners even if they are so called "illegal". **You will lose anything but gain happiness and attract many blessings for yourself!**

In whatever I did for him I was not expecting anything from him. I wanted just his success in a foreign land where there are the human beings like him. His brothers and sisters. I did not care that his visa was expired.

I knew that what I was doing with my friends God was with me and if God is with you who can be against you? My Cameroonian friend was a human being who needed to live among us. He was a person who came in Burundi to harm my beloved and great Burundian people.

Most of the laws we create are not just and right with God that is why a strong people may oppress the weak using the law. If any law is against any innocent human being then it is against God himself! There is a time you fear God than a human being when the good cause is there. If you fear to support such a life due to fear you may find yourself losing your life. Because such a life is Jesus in person and if you refuse to do anything to save that life and remain comfortable instead of taking action even if it is highly risky and choose silence; God will still help that person with or without you but to you there is a word against you spoken by Jesus when His majesty Jesus Christ said:" **Those who love their life in this world will lose it. Those who care nothing for their life in this world will keep it for eternity." John 12:25, New Living Translation.**

One day I said to my beloved friend that where there is a high good risk, there is a high glory! If you are looking greatness, there is a price you have to pay. Our wonderful God and Father Jesus Christ have already done everything we need. He has already overcome for us but with your courage and faith in Him, you may remain the same! Maybe what you are looking for is in the mouth of the lion and, I am sorry to say that but you will have to use courage to get what is yours.

A young man one day came and found his beloved people in front of an enemy sure of himself. His people were only singing that we shall overcome but refuse to pay the price that was needed to get their victory.

That situation went on about 40 days. No one was willing to pay the price but they loved their life including their king Saul. But when that small but great boy David appeared there, he put on courage and faith in His God who is always faithful in His promises.

David dared to pay the price and attack which gave him fame and glory and fear among His people and enemies. It was a good cause that demanded to hate his life to save his people and earn the glory for the name of the Lord!

To all who are in Christ, We are descendants of the Lion of Judah; let's therefore behave likewise, like lions! Our forefathers, Judah, David king and Jesus Christ himself the God of gods are our witnesses. There is no excuse of not winning in our different ways toward our destiny!

 You know what? For my beloved human being like me from Cameroon I managed to get more than 1000% through him if I calculate the money I used to give him and what I received through him without any expectation from him. I supported him morally, spiritually and financially cheerfully according to the word of God. I saw the man like Jesus not like but like a brother, a God sent person for Burundi.

I am a witness among many other people who experienced the benefit hidden in helping others not matter how risky it is.

It is time for America , Europe, China to help Africa and every part of our world to develop themselves without expecting anything but I am telling you the truth that you will be rewarded somehow. It is a spiritual law whether you expect a reward or not you will still receive a reward but support others as a desire to see other people around you improving their lives. God is faithful.

Let it be a culture all over the world in Jesus mighty name!

Take care of the so called dreamers as yourself, you will never go wrong. Love them; protect them as your own people because they are truly your own people since they are human beings like you! Jesus Christ the God of gods promised in **Luke 6:38** Amplified Bible (AMP):"

Give and it will be given to you. They will pour into your lap a good measure—pressed down, shaken together and running over [with no space left for more]. For with the standard of measurement you use [when you do good to others], it will be measured to you in return."

People like to give in churches and forget those surrounding them in need. They even forget their parents but rush giving in churches. They do not know that JESUS IS IN EVERYONE THEY MEET IN NEED. I am not telling you not to give in our churches because myself I do but we should not forget what God says that matters. Look what Jesus said: "**Woe to you, teachers of the law and Pharisees, you hypocrites! You give a tenth of your spices—mint, dill and cumin. But you have neglected the more important matters of the law—justice, mercy and** faithfulness. You should have practiced the latter, without neglecting the former."Matthew 23Matthew23:23, New International Version.

What God was saying about Mercy, faith and Justice? It is about to take care of those in need like widow, fatherless, foreigner;…Look in **Deuteronomy26:12-15:" When you have finished setting aside a tenth of all your produce in the third year, the year of the tithe, you shall give it to the** *Levite (Like pastor or a priest), the foreigner, the fatherless and the widow,* **so that they may eat in your towns and be satisfied.**

Then say to the Lord your God: "I have removed from my house the sacred portion and have given it to the Levite, the foreigner, the fatherless and the widow, according to all you commanded.

I have not turned aside from your commands nor have I forgotten any of them. I have not eaten any of the sacred portion while I was in mourning, nor have I removed any of it while I was unclean, nor have I offered any of it to the dead.

I have obeyed the Lord my God; I have done everything you commanded me. [15] Look down from heaven, your holy dwelling place, and bless your people Israel and the land you have given us as you promised on oath to our ancestors, a land flowing with milk and honey.", New International Version.

You can read Matthew 25Matthew25:34-46, New International Version to see how Jesus cerebrated those who put their faith in action through doing good to those in need. It is like God is hidden in those people in need you do not want to greet or to invite for a dinner. May the Lord help us!

[34] "Then the King will say to those on his right, 'Come, you who are blessed by my Father; take your inheritance, the kingdom prepared for you since the creation of the world. [35] For I was hungry and you gave me something to eat, I was thirsty and you gave me something to drink, I was a stranger and you invited me in, [36] I needed clothes and you clothed me, I was sick and you looked after me, I was in prison and you came to visit me.'

[37] "Then the righteous will answer him, 'Lord, when did we see you hungry and feed you, or thirsty and give you something to drink? [38] When did we see you a stranger and invite you in or needing clothes and clothe you? [39] When did we see you sick or in prison and go to visit you?'

[40] "The King will reply, 'Truly I tell you, whatever you did for one of the least of these brothers and sisters of mine, you did for me.'

[41] "Then he will say to those on his left, 'Depart from me, you who are cursed, into the eternal fire prepared for the devil and his angels. [42] For I was hungry and you gave me nothing to eat, I was thirsty and you gave me nothing to drink, [43] I was a stranger and you did not invite me in, I needed clothes and you did not clothe me, I was sick and in prison and you did not look after me.'

[44] "They also will answer, 'Lord, when did we see you hungry or thirsty or a stranger or needing clothes or sick or in prison, and did not help you?'

[45] "He will reply, 'Truly I tell you, whatever you did not do for one of the least of these; you did not do for me.'

[46] "Then they will go away to eternal punishment, but the righteous to eternal life."

When you want to help them also consider their honor they deserve. Remember those people you meet are "temples" of God. Take care of the members of your families. Your neighbor is asking you 1000 US to finance his project and you are sure he is going to succeed if you help him.

If you are not helping those in need around you and rush to give in church while someone was supported to be helped by you ,then I think your gift will not benefit you. You are wasting your time and energy. Never underestimate the cry behind you that is against you no matter how anointed you think you are!

Our Holy and God the everlasting Father Jesus Christ said:" …Therefore if you are offering your gift at the altar and there remember that your brother has something against you, **leave your gift there before the altar. First go and be reconciled to your brother; then and offer your gift." Matthew 5:23-24.**

In the case of helping it means, first take care of the people that needed your care and then go and give without any cry behind your back. For example if you are enjoying life and forget your parents and family, instead of long life that you expect, it will be a short life.

In order words, it may be a short prosperity, you are amassing wealth but something will happen to take away your hard earned money no matter how intelligent you are.

A curse that you deserve will always work against you until you rectify your errors. The only solution to remove a curse is through the blood of Jesus for forgiveness before God but you need also to rectify before a man in case you behaved wrongly before a man. That is what Zacchaeus did. "But Zacchaeus stood up and said to the Lord, **"Look, Lord, half of my possessions I give** to the poor, and if I have cheated anyone, I will repay it fourfold." Jesus said to him, "Today salvation has come to this house, because this man too is a son of Abraham." Luke 19:8-9.

See what Jesus is answering you:" **Jesus replied, "And why do you break the command of God for the sake of your tradition? [4] For God said, 'Honor your father and mother' and 'anyone who curses their father or mother is to be put to death.' [5] But you say that if anyone declares that what might have been used to help their father or mother is 'devoted to God,' [6] they are not to 'honor their father or mother' with it. Thus you nullify the word of God for the sake of your tradition. [7] You hypocrites! Isaiah was right when he prophesied about you:**

"'These people honor me with their lips, but their hearts are far from me. [9] They worship me in vain; their teachings are merely human rules." Matthew 15Matthew15:3-9 New International Version.

People do not understand that to the best way to cloth the naked, to feed the hungry and so is to give them a job in what they like because if they are doing what they do not like they might produce negative results. I believe that a frustrated man will always produce frustrated results.

Do what I did to my beloved friend so called foreigner when I looked for him a job. He would buy for himself whatever he wished. That is the best way to feed, to clothe the naked and so. Use your connections or whatever you have in your hands to make sure your fellow human being like you is happy.

To men of God, you should watch to not behave like the priest and the Levite in the parable of good Samaritan rather you should be the first to practice mercy. Understand well where God is.

"For   I   desire   mercy,   not   sacrifice,

and acknowledgment of God rather than burnt offerings." Hosea 6:6 New International

Version.

Beloved people from all over the world, I have seen that it is far better to love, and help those in need around you. Take care the so called foreigners and God will bless you!

5. Miraculously rise of the price of Bitcoin

Nothing happen by accident, there is always something that causes things to happen!

"Lord, you promised me that you will show your power to the nations through me. Can you please show to me how great you are in the financial realm in rising up the price of Bitcoin in one year?" This is the prayer I prayed when one bitcoin costed around 770$ in 2015.

Our God liked people who asked Him signs. He told King **Ahaz**:" Again the LORD spoke to Ahaz: **"Ask for a sign from the LORD your God, whether from the depths of Sheol or the heights of heaven."** Isaiah 38:21-22.

Remember I had already asked and received an everlasting covenant with my God with the promises of King David as promised in Isaiah 55:3-5:" Incline your ear, and come unto me: hear, and your soul shall live; and **I will make an everlasting covenant with you, even the sure mercies of David.**

[4] **Behold, I have given him for a witness to the people, a leader and commander to the people.**

[5] **Behold, thou shalt call a nation that thou knowest not, and nations that knew not thee shall run unto thee because of the Lord thy God, and for the Holy One of Israel; for he hath glorified thee."**

Our wonderful friend at all times and forever who is mighty God and everlasting Father Himself Jesus Christ said:" **When you ask believe you have received".**

So, I knew I had already received the promise but I wanted to be persuaded through a sign from my beloved and Almighty God my heavenly Father. That is why I prayed to my God **who is, who was and who is about to come** and said:" **Let one bitcoin goes up to 10,000 US$ in one year between 2016 and 2017. I know you can do that and even do exceedingly above all I ask and imagine In the name of Jesus Christ!"** I wanted to see the power of our heavenly Father in financial realm.

God always give signs to his chosen ones to prove to them and remove every doubt that He is with them. He did it to Gideon, King Saul… When someone is not really persuaded of what he believes in; it is easy to lose focus and give up when trials and tribulations arise. I did know how our great God can do that. What I knew everything is possible with God according to the King of kings Jesus Christ.

Can I tell you that in one year the bitcoin was almost $20,000 a coin in December 2017? I could not believe what was happening when I looked on the screen one day in December 2017 watching myself news on.

What is impossible with God? I praise my Lord Jesus Christ, my Almighty God, my Father and the Rock of my salvation for such grace and favor toward me. He humbled himself and granted me my request because He loves me.

He has put His great trust in me and chosen me like one of His great vessel King David He used to establish His kingdom on earth. He has showed to me His power just to let me know that He has made with me an everlasting covenant and given me the promises of King David.

My Lord Jesus Christ knew before the foundation of the world that I am able to carry out this noble cause of being like my father through faith in Christ King David.

Thank you Jesus Christ and my Heavenly Father for your amazing grace. Allow me oh God and receive my humble" I love you" from your beloved son.

If you are interested Here's a look back at bitcoin's journey in 2017:

From $900 to $20,000: Bitcoin's Historic 2017 Price Run Revisited (https://www.coindesk.com/900-20000-bitcoins-historic-2017-price-run-revisited).

One year ago as of the time of writing, the price of bitcoin traded between $930 and $978 — movements that perhaps set the stage for the cryptocurrency's value to cross the $1,000 on New

Year's Day. Indeed, that headline-making development would be the first of many to come for 2017.

In this article, we look at some of the major moments for bitcoin's price during the last 12 months, a period of time that saw the price of bitcoin climb from below $1,000 to nearly $20,000 on the CoinDesk Bitcoin Price Index (BPI).

It was a year that arguably exceeded last year's bullish predictions and one that saw unprecedented interest coming from places – particularly in the finance industry – that some may not have imagined possible just 12 months ago.

The PBOC impact

While January started off with bitcoin price fireworks, that month would also see one of the defining regulatory moments of 2017: an initial move by the People's Bank of China, the country's central bank, to tighten its oversight of the country's then-dominant bitcoin exchanges.

Yet, the warnings from Chinese officials didn't cause the market death blow that some observers feared.

However, it did lead to a drop in trading volume as a result of the imposition of new trading fees by what were then the "Big Three" exchanges – Huobi, OKCoin and BTCC. Those exchanges later halted withdrawals following new edicts from the PBoC, ultimately closing fiat trading this fall following further restrictions from Chinese regulators.

The 'no' heard round the world

Investors Cameron and Tyler Winklevoss first filed to launch a bitcoin exchange-traded fund back in 2013, setting the stage for a multi-year journey that led to the March 2017 rejection by the U.S. Securities and Exchange Commission (SEC).

And while the SEC has since moved to review that decision – a process that is still pending – markets at the time reacted poorly, perhaps because some were betting that the U.S. regulator would approve rather than shoot down the proposed ETF.

On the news, the market dropped by nearly 30% that day, ultimately recovering above the $1,000 level after the initial drop.

But in what was perhaps a harbinger of the months to come, bitcoin's price was back above its pre-ETF point within days of the ruling. And despite the reluctance expressed by the SEC at the time, a number of firms have filed tofiledto create bitcoin ETFs, with a particular focus on funds tied to cryptocurrency futures.

The summer of bulls

If there was one phrase to define the period between May and September of this year, it was this: a new all-time high for bitcoin.

The cryptocurrencycryptocurrency's price pushed past each successive milestone with apparent ease, including one on May 1 that saw bitcoin break past a record set on an infamous and now-defunct exchange.

This summer also saw significant activity around initial coin offerings, as shown by data in CoinDeskCoinDesk's ICO Tracker, leading one observer to dub it "the summer of crypto love."

As May drew to a close, the price of bitcoin climbed above $2,000 for the first time and surpassed $3,000 just weeks later. At the same time, those price milestones were often accompanied by subsequent turbulence, including aincludinga drop of $300 within one hour just a day after the $3,000 line was first crossed.

Perhaps one of the most noteworthy developments was the entry of major Wall Street analysts to the bitcoin price-watching game. Goldman Sach's Sheba Jafari notably predicted the move past $4,000, leading to further forecasts from both Goldman Sachs and other analysts as the weeks and months progressed.

By the first week of September, the price of bitcoin exceeded $5,000 for the first time – only to drop by hundreds of dollars two days later. Indeed, the coming days would see a reversal of the late summer's gains, with the cryptocurrency's price falling below $3,400 on Sep. 14 and down past $3,000 the following day.

Past $10,000 and beyond

By mid-October, the September malaise had been forgotten and the price of bitcoin was once again above $5,000.

Despite the pending closure of China's "Big Three" exchanges and a global crackdown on unregulated ICOs beginning to take shape, the price of bitcoin was largely buoyed by a bullish sentiment which would set the stage for some of the eye-popping moves in store for November and December.

Yet for all the regulatory rumblings and forks away from the bitcoin network, the cryptocurrency's price largely continued its upward trajectory, culminating with the CoinDesk Bitcoin Price IndexIndex's all-time high of $19,783.21 on Dec. 17.

I was choked to see How that thing was done. Nothing is impossible with God. Our God is awesome; there is no one like Him. He deserves our thanksgiving and love by doing His good and wonderful commandments.

After that I said:" Thank you my God for showing me your power even in the money field. Can you now bring it back?" The Lord did it!

The downfall of Bitcoin was seen according to **https://www.coindesk.com/900-20000-bitcoins-historic-2017-price-run-revisited**: "That close encounter with $20,000 was followed just days later by a 30% drop that shaved billions of dollars off of the total crypto currency market capitalization. It was one of the biggest market corrections seen to date, sending bitcoin's price tumbling below $11,000.

Over the coming days, the price of bitcoin would recover, climbing back beyond $16,000 and higher on other cryptocurrency exchanges worldwide. Yet as shown in the most recent graphs and price data, bitcoin's value has begun falling, dropping to the mid-$13k's on Dec. 28 after opening the day above $15,000."

Today 3/21/2019 bitcoin price is $4,088.37. **I HAVE SEEN MY God** in the financial realm. Whether Bitcoin rises again I do not know. It will depend on God's. People should fear and honor our God in the name of Jesus. He is the master of everything. He is in control forever above everything created. He is in control of economy or every affairs of a man.

My God showed me His power according to His promise. He is going also to establish me as the King of all nations in His wonderful name for His glory. He promised me that He will cause nations to honor me. If God is for me, who can be against me? Glory to my beloved Lord Jesus Christ and heavenly Father! Blessed are people who will support me from the least the great, from the poor to the rich from all over the world.

Let everything He created worship and praise Him because of His power and greatness that last forever!

Do want to know Another example of the True of His word?

Do you remember that the Lord Jesus Christ has granted me the blessings He promised to King David?

Let me show you again some of his promises given to King David in his time that are now mine in the glorious and mighty name of Jesus Christ the Savior of the Humanity.

Psalm 89:20-37 Amplified Bible (AMP)

20 "I have found David My servant; With My holy oil I have anointed him,
21 With whom My hand shall be established and steadfast; My arm also shall strengthen him.
22 "The enemy will not outwit him, nor will the wicked man afflict or humiliate him.
23 "I will crush his adversaries before him, And strike (plague in King James Version; Kill in Good News Translation; smite which means "to hit someone forcefully or to have a sudden powerful or damaging effect on someone" according to Cambridge Dictionary) in American Standard Version) those who hate him.

24 "My faithfulness and My steadfast loving-kindness shall be with him, And in My name shall his horn be exalted [great power and prosperity shall be conferred upon him].
25 "I will also [a]set his hand on the [Mediterranean] sea, And his right hand on the rivers [the tributaries of the Euphrates].
26 "He will cry to Me, 'You are my Father, My God, and the rock of my salvation.'
27 "I will also make him My firstborn (preeminent), The highest of the kings of the earth.

28 "My loving-kindness I will keep for him forevermore, And My covenant will be confirmed to him.

29 "His descendants I will establish forever, And his throne [will endure] as the days of heaven.

30 "If his children [b]turn away from My law And do not walk in My ordinances,

31 If they break My statutes And do not keep My commandments,

32 Then I will punish their transgression with the rod [of discipline],And [correct] their wickedness with stripes.

33 Nevertheless, I will not break off My loving kindness from him, Nor allow My faithfulness to fail.

34 "My covenant I will not violate, Nor will I alter the utterance of My lips.

35 "Once [for all] I have sworn by My holiness, [My vow which cannot be violated]; I will not lie to David.

36 "His [c]descendants shall endure forever And his throne [will continue] as the sun before Me.

37 "It shall be established forever like the moon, And the witness in the heavens is ever faithful." Selah.

Footnotes:

1.   Psalm 89:25 I.e. extends his area of influence.

2.   Psalm 89:30 Lit forsake.

3.   Psalm 89:36 Lit seed.

Wait and do not be tired because I want to show you that the God of Moses, who is the God of David, is **the same yesterday, today and forever** in the way He keeps every word He promises. And that is in the name of Jesus Christ.

The example is about how God plagued his enemies.

What did Jesus Christ the God almighty did in plaguing those who were against his purpose? Let me tell you briefly 2 examples one with Moses and another one with David King:

1. In the time of Moses, Jesus Christ plagued Pharaoh who was refusing to let his people to leave Egypt. God's purpose in sending the ten plagues upon Egypt was to force Pharaoh the Hebrews free and allow them to worship God.

The 10 plagues can be found in the Bible from Exodus 7:14 to Exodus 12:36.

List of the ten plagues according to **https://www.bibleinfo.com/en/questions/what-are-10-plagues-egypt#blood**

1.   Blood

2.   Frogs

3.   Lice or gnats

4.   Flies

5.   Livestock

6.   Boils

7.   Hail

8.   Locust

9.   Darkness

10.   Death of firstborn

The king of Egypt finally left his people alone and started their long journey toward their promised land. Today Jehovah is revealed in the name of Jesus Christ. And because Jesus is just He punishes. You have been often taught Jesus as a lamb of God but also remember that He is the Lion of Judah. And today, Jesus is on throne with the Church. Doing what? Judging nations and guiding the world in His righteous ways!

2. In the time of David, the king of Israel.

Jesus Christ the Creator of the Universe the one who was backing Moses is the same one Who promised David to protect him because he was on his mission hence David king would pray;"

You give great victories to your king; you show unfailing love to your anointed, to David and all his descendants forever." 2 Samuel 22:51, New Living Translation.

David knew that Jesus Christ was ruling Israel through Him. Those promises were sword to guard and protect his chosen king David in his generation and in my generation. How? yes because our beloved Lord, savior, protector and God, Everlasting Father and mighty God Jesus Christ is the same yesterday, and today, and forever ." Hebrews 13:8 King James Version (KJV).

Jesus is saying now to you that" **Repent therefore! Otherwise, I will soon come to you and will fight against them with the sword of my mouth.**" Revelation 2:16, New International Version.

His Sword is more dangerous than the nuclear weapon. My beloved people from all over the world we have to fear our God who is our only maker and love Him as sons and daughters. He loves us but because He is just He also punishes people who refuse to repent.

In the time of King David Jesus Christ killed someone called Nabal who was able to help David in his mission but refused to help him though David did good things to him and God killed him himself, how ? He plagued him with probably a stroke (*A stroke occurs when the blood supply to part of your brain is interrupted or reduced, depriving brain tissue of oxygen and nutrients. Within minutes, brain cells begin to die. A stroke is a medical emergency*) and the man died (1 Samuel 251Samuel25:1-38).

Moses did not have a physical army like pharaoh with him but he was more powerful than pharaoh because God the creator of pharaoh was backing him up. It matters who is backing you! It is said:"**The king is not saved by the great size of his army; A warrior is not rescued by his great strength. A horse is a false hope for victory; Nor does it deliver anyone by its great strength.**" Psalm33:17, Amplified Bible version.

 In order words, the King can win with or without a great army as long as the king is supported by the Creator of the Universe, the good God.

God arms his people under his mission with weapons that are more powerful than any weapon on Earth. His weapons are more powerful than a sword, guns, nuclear weapon or any human weapons.

Which are those divine weapons? His promises of course which are like fire, a hammer:**"Is not my word like fire," declares the LORD, "and like a hammer that breaks a rock in pieces?** Jeremiah 23:29, New International Version; or **"this is what the LORD God Almighty says: "***Because the people have spoken these words, I will make my words in your mouth a fire and these people the wood it consumes.* Jeremiah5:14, New international Version;

Moreover **"no** *weapon forged against you will prevail, and you will refute every tongue that accuses you. This is the heritage of the servants of the LORD, and this is their vindication from me," declares the LORD.*" Isaiah54:17, New translation Version.

Or **"There is no wisdom nor understanding nor counsel against Yahweh." Proverbs 21:30, World English Bible** .

I have already said what was said about David and his helpers like:"Peace and prosperity be with you, and success to all who help you, for your God is the one who helps you." In 1Chronicles12:18, New Living Translation.

You know what? If there is a success for those who help DAVID HIS King because he has come in the name of the Lord then there is no success to those who refuse to help me yet they are able to help his king.

We have already seen in the life of David when Nabal who was rich refused to help King David how God killed Nabal using a fatal disease.

I have already told you how someone who helped me with some money in Zambia got 5 times the money she helped me with in less than 30 minutes. I remember praying to the Lord:" If you have given me the promises of King David, then make everyone who help me see a success immediately!"

After that prayer a friend of mine would see something happen in his life almost immediately after helping me with something I needed until he vowed to always supporting me when he is able to help me. Our GOD is good and faithful.

In the opposite, I saw a man who was refusing to do for me what he promised to me and giving some reason. I tried to explain to him that if he chooses to keep the word, God will make him prosperous but he refused.

*And I prayed to my God, the King of kings and Lord f lords:"***Lord I was trying to help my friend to be faithful, please teach him to be faithful and prove me right***.*

The Lord stopped what he was expecting to get from his boss although it was a promise. Later on, the same person blessed me with something and I prayed for God to give him a better job where he will get more money than what he lost. In one month, he got a better job. Praise be to the Lord!

People must know how to kiss the son! It is written in **Psalm2:10-12** says, "Therefore, you kings, be wise; be warned, you rulers of the earth. Serve the LORD with fear and celebrate his rule with trembling. **Kiss his son**, or he will be angry and your way will lead to your destruction, for his wrath can flare up in a moment. Blessed are all who take refuge in him." The hearers of this psalm were to "kiss his son" or submit to the Lord to keep Him from becoming angry with them.

The NLT translates the phrase as "**Submit to God's royal son**," and the NASB says, "**Do homage to the Son**."

Have I seen people punished by God who were trying to harm me? Yes, and the following is an example.

One man with whom I was sharing a room in a certain guest room in a certain country tried to stop me from entering the room. He locked the room and I was tired and I wanted to rest.

I told him please open the room but he refused. Immediately I felt angry and I said:" Lord Jesus you told me you have given me the promises of David in my time as your king over all the Earth. If I am really your king please proves it against this man because one of the promises you did to David is to plague his haters. I want to see that you are with me and that you stand for your words.

Gideon in his time asked to God many signs for God to prove that He was Him who was sending Gideon to fight against the enemies of Israel. For me it was another sign I was asking to my God and He answered me.

Do you know what happened to that man?

*Early in the morning, the man was humble before me, calm and I was wondering what happened. And he told me: "Doctor, I have just lost my Aunt the only one who was remaining and cared for me as my own mother (his biological mother was already late)." That morning I beheld how God is **faithful in all his promises**. Our God must be feared and He is about to make sure all the world respects and honors him as God alone.*

After seeing that, I asked God to forgive him and never punishes like that because he was doing what he does not know. He did know who he was fighting against.

Beloved people from all over the World, please let fear our God, Jesus Christ, the Lion of Judah because there is a time that he acts as a lion not like a lamb. He always makes sure all his promises are true forever. He is a loving God but he is also terrible to those against him.

It is written in Psalm2:12 in different versions

"Submit to God's royal son, or he will become angry, and you will be destroyed in the midst of all your activities--for his anger flares up in an instant. But what joy for all who take refuge in him!" New Living Translation

or

"Show respect to his son because if you don't, the LORD might become furious and suddenly destroy you. But he blesses and protects everyone who runs to him.'' Contemporary English Version

Or "Kiss the son before he becomes angry, and you die where you stand. Indeed, his wrath can flare up quickly. How blessed are those who take refuge in him." International Standard Version.

In 1 Samuel 221Samuel22:22-23 because David knew that he was with God he was sure that whoever is with him was safe. That what he told Abiathar: " Stay with me; do not be afraid, for he who seeks my life seeks your life, but you are safe with me."

6. The power through the name of the Lord Jesus Christ

The Lord God promised David that he shall have great power through His name or "My faithfulness and gracious love will be with him, and **in my name his power will be exalted"** in **Psalm 89:24 International Standard Version.**

The Lord showed me the power in His name!

A Certain man with whom I was staying at home wanted to harm me! He said something that I like to make men of God my friends. I said yes supported by what King David said: "Those who serve the Lord will be my friend." I am like David, therefore I like every word David said.

He said:" you are sick!" I said no but I am healthy. I am a medical doctor I knew what I was saying I did not to insult him because it is not right with God. I refused to say amen to his curse and confessed a blessing. The devil will never allow you to have good things for you but you have to fight through faith in the name of our wonderful and only true God Christ Jesus.

He commanded me to go to sleep. I told him that I am not a boy. He should respect me! He tried to make me move by force. I shouted leave alone but he continued. I do not like to fight with people. I like peace with everybody. Then I shouted in that night:" Do not touch me again in the name of Jesus Christ! Immediately something pushed me out of me.

I tried to analyze his behavior and I was told that he used to be

The Word of God is powerful and can never miss his target. I remember one day I was working for a certain company. They refused to pay me. And they wanted me to stop working from that place. I became angry and I said:" I declare judgment over the company. I told one of the employees that the company is going to close! That cannot be possible! He said. But after one or two weeks the company closed and they lost a lot of money.

It is written:" Kiss his son, or he will be angry and your way will lead to your destruction, for his wrath can flare up in a moment. Blessed are all who take refuge in him."Psalm 2Psalm2:12, New International Version.

The Lord has made my words as sharp as a sword like what is written:" He made my mouth like a sharpened sword, in the shadow of his hand he hid me; he made me into a polished arrow and concealed me in his quiver." Isaiah 49Isaiah49:2, New International Version.

You   can   read   also   in:"
Isaiah   11:4
but with righteousness He will judge the poor, and with equity He will decide in favor of the earth's oppressed. He will strike the earth with the rod of His mouth and slay the wicked with the breath of His lips;

Revelation   2:16
Therefore repent! Otherwise I will come to you shortly and wage war against them with the sword of My mouth."

 These words are true! The word of God does work all over the world.

Through the mighty name of Jesus Christ I won some battles.

Let me tell you about what happened before the end of Osama Ben Laden and Trump Victory.

1. The end of Osama Ben Laden

One of the promises the Lord gave me is to possess the key of David. The Bible says in **Zechariah12:8** that the house of David will lead the people like Angel of God, like God himself in order words like Jesus Christ himself.

It is written in revelation that Jesus is holy, true, and whatever He opens, no one can shut, and what He shuts no one can open. Again Jesus rules with great power, absolute power. I understood that as the firstborn of God on earth I will be ruling in his name with great power and using the keys of David.

Then how God rules? In Psalm89:14 we read the character of God:" *Righteousness and justice are the foundation of your throne; love and faithfulness go before you.*" **New International Version**.

The leadership of angel of God to the place prepared by God: He protects the people; the people must pay attention to him and obey him since sent by God he does not pardon rebellion.

How did I use the key of David I understood that when God has given you something it is already there that is why He said believe that you have already received whatever you ask for. That means in Heaven they know they have already a King over all the Earth who comes in the name of Jesus. When I gave myself to our beloved Heavenly Father in the name of Jesus Christ, I said:" **Lord here I am, send me Lord I am ready to rule the whole world like your David king in my time**"

After that The Holy Spirit led to a verse I had not yet known before written in **Zechariah14.9**: "**The Lord will be king over the whole earth. On that day there will be one Lord, and his name the only name.**" **New International Version**. When I saw this prophecy I realized I am under a divine mission to fulfill this prophecy.

Again, it is written in **Zechariah13.2**: "**On that day, I will banish the names of the idols from the land, and they will be remembered no more,**" declares **the Lord Almighty. "I will remove both the prophets and the spirit of impurity from the land. New International Version**.

I had vowed to my God to make sure the world is Holy to the Lord. In the time Of David the throne of David was also a throne of God; His kingdom was The Lord's. That is why God said I watch over your kingdom; why? Because it was His. So the success of the David in what right in the eyes of God was God's; therefore it was impossible to fail for David. The Lord made sure he succeeded where he went and became more powerful than his enemies.

In psalm 2:8-9, the Lord God asked David his king: "**If you ask, I will give you nations, everyone will be yours. You will rule them with great power, you will scatter your enemies like broken pieces of pottery.**"

I remember one day I said my dear Lord Jesus Christ, I believe in every word you have written or say. That is why I said that I have asked nations and they are mine they are my people and I started loving and praying for all nations as my beloved people.

I started following what is happening around our dear globe. I intercede for the world as my own people as one people. I pray against diseases that are against my people from all over the world like cancer,….

When others are busy praying for their own nation, my concern is the whole world.

Then, In 2001, right on our Television, what was happening was horrible: The 9/11, the "black" day to USA. The great nation in the world full of intelligent people, full of nuclear weapons and all kind of arms was beaten and hit by mere human beings.

The bible says "*If the LORD does not build the house; it is useless for the builders to work on it. If the LORD does not protect a city, it is useless for the guard to stay alert.*" **Psalm 127:1 (GW)**

It was not an attack only to USA but to the Whole world.

So attack America meant to attack me it is like to attack Israel as well. I love America and I love Israel too.

So, in my room I said Lord, if you gave me the key of David: what I open no one can shut what I shut no one can open.

This a prayer that I used to confess even when I am with others, and one of my friend told me : It is not what you are asking that everybody can ask there is something what God has put on your heart that will be your own burden but not for everybody. I remember what the Savior of the Whole World said: "**You cannot receive this saying unless, to whom it is given.** " **Matthew19.11.**

Then I prayed America is like to attack Christianity, those who attacked America came in the name of a religion; and then I said: Lord Jesus let Ben Laden be captured by America. If America wins it is Christ who wins, but if not then Islam would think they won. I SHOUTED: "IN THE NAME OF Jesus Christ I arrest Ben Laden!"

Ben Laden was not captured because of our intelligent soldiers or because of the American most advanced military technologies but because of God.

My beloved and great Mr. Obama was pushed by a hand behind the scene: **The Hand of God**. They were not sure of victory. I am writing this so that people give back the glory to God.

I advice all my beloved human beings liked me who are in Islam to love Christ Jesus like their God and Savior. Only him He is worthy of worship all over the World!

2. The victory of Mr Donald Trump in the US general presidential elections.

During 2016 US elections this great woman Hillary Clinton had a bigger support than Trump. Hillary was supported by Obama. Hillary had a lot of Money in her campaign more than Trump. Hillary had the main media behind her while Trump was not. He chose to use Facebook and Tweeter for His Campaign.

I like Obama but I hated what He did in supporting homosexuality instead of helping our beloved people under the bad spirit of homosexuality to get rid of it so that instead of adopting children due to the instinct created in them of having children but through heterosexuality.

They are able to get married and get their own children without of course to adopt some orphans which also a good thing.

Homosexuality is a serious problem and the world must fix it. When you support a sin you became weak. Hillary was not saying against homosexuality meaning she was going to continue what Obama was doing.

I respect her as a great mother and I remember rebuking a friend of mine who was publishing something on facebook against her in insulting way. I told her you should respect her in while posting what you do not like about her.

Freedom of speech is not freedom of insulting your leaders. We have to be careful how we talk against our leaders I told her "Hillary Clinton is a great mother though she can have some weakness as a human being. I may not agree with a stand of someone but still respect and love the person. I did not like her support to Homosexuality because God is against that. Whatever our God in whom America trusts is against to; we must be against as well to that.

Obama is married to his lovely wife Michelle Obama why fight and help others who are in the wrong way to become normal like him?

I read on internet that if you support homosexuality vote Hillary but if not vote Trump.

I said: **"Lord Trump must win in the name of Jesus Christ. If you made the first born of all rulers oh Lord, then I allow Trump to win."**

I started following polls. When I was praying Trump would go up in the polls but when not praying Hillary, that courageous and strong lady would lead the polls.

That reminded me what happened with Moses whenever he would raise his hands in prayer Israel would win by the hand of Joshua; but when not the enemy would lead the battle.

Moses was on the mountain praying while Joshua was the commander in army on the ground but all eyes were on Moses. Aaron, the brother to Moses realized that and put Moses on a stone and help Moses to hold his hands up until the total victory.

When I realized how things were going on; I started praying continually until the day before the general elections. Trump won because God was for him. My beloved people in Democrats were surprised of the victory. They think it is the president Putin of my beloved great people of Russia who became wiser than Obama in refusing homosexuality that Obama was supporting that enabled Trump to win.

It is Jesus Christ was against you! Homosexuality is a serious sin that brings a curse to people and defile the earth and whoever is supporting it is an enemy of the people because he is helping them to their auto destruction. You are annihilating their future generation in them. Jesus is the same in the time of Sodom and Gomorrah, today and forever. I love Obama he is courageous brilliant, intelligent but I did not like his support to homosexuality; same thing I love and respect Hillary Clinton as my mother but I did not like her position to homosexuality.

But do you know there is a reward to people who follows and support the righteousness of God? When you support the ways of God, He will support you; therefore He will make you stronger in your life. **A sin always cheapens someone!** It makes a sinful man weak!

Jesus Christ the Savior of the Earth said that "happy are those who are pure in the heart for they shall see God" meaning they shall experience the miraculous salvation from God, they shall see his power in their life.

I am a witness for that how righteousness benefit everyone who practices it! Do you want to know about my experience? :

When I reached Zambia, my visa was about to expire, I rushed to the border to renew my visa. The government had already given me a letter that allow me to serve my beloved great Zambian people as their medical doctor but an immigration officer wanted me to give them some money. For what? Corruption?

''If you don't have the money then I will put you in jail!'' The chief intimidated me. I told him I do not have the money they wanted me to give them.

They were working for the government of this great man, a man I love who declared October 18th of every year a "national prayer day", the president Edgar C. Lungu.

They wanted me to give them $300 and they pushed me to pay them quickly otherwise the following day I would pay $400. You know what? The $300 was the exact money for the license from the healthy profession council of Zambia.

A friend of mine had already promised to pay that money for the license. When they heard there is someone who is ready to pay that money, they told me to call him and bring them the money.

I called my friend and he said that he was going to come the following day. They told me:" while we are waiting for your friend we are going to put in a hotel."

But, the chief called and told me:" Here there is no comedy, you pay the money or we put you in jail!"

"Sir, I told you I do not have money now but if the Lord God allows you to put me in jail pleases do it! "I replied him fixing my eyes to him without fear.

"I am done", the chief commanded a woman immigration officer who tried to look for a way to save me from the chief but in vain.

They put me in a police cell with other Zambians who were there some because of a crime they committed and other foreigners who were there because they entered Zambia without passport, without visa.

An immigration officer who took me to the cell told me He is going to put in the cell while they are waiting for the money.

"It is a command from the chief otherwise you do not deserve the cell." The immigration officer explained to me.

Once in the cell they started getting a lot of food from different people more than what they were getting before me.

"Doctor abwera bwino (meaning This doctor has Come with good things)!"One of my friends in the cell told his friend using the Zambian local language.

This is the same thing my beloved Aunt and her great husband told me once I was already in Zambia. They told me that I was a blessing to them while I was staying with them.

I stayed with them for many years up to the day I left Burundi to Zambia. Her husband, a great man that I love prayed for me the night before I left Burundi. That unforgettable night tears came out of my eyes. I was going to miss them!

My dearest biological father told me you are "Nizigiyimana" (meaning in God I trust) God will be with you! I am grateful to my dearest wonderful and Almighty heavenly Father for choosing my father and mother as my biological father and mother! My father is a man of faith!

What they said what the Lord Jesus promised me in **Psalm72: 17, New International Version:"May his name endure forever;**

may it continue as long as the sun. Then all nations will be blessed through him, and they will call him blessed."

When I was in the cell people told me that pray God that the your Zambian friend come quickly otherwise you will go in the court after some 1 or 2 months like us and you are not going to win in the court because you are a foreigner.

In my heart I said that whether my friend comes or not I will come out of the cell as a free man.

I prayed:**" remember my God that I have been praying for Zambia as my own people starting to the president Lungu;**

Remember also I did not commit adultery when that man wanted to pay for me a prostitute woman in Zambia because it was a sin to you (although there is a pleasure to commit

adultery or but it is not a good pleasure at all. It is something that takes someone to auto destruction. Sin will always cheapen you!)

Therefore my God; do not allow them to put me in court and let me leave this cell as a free man without any handcuffs on my hands."

Another thing in the in the cell it was hot. I wanted to bath but there was no water. The only water that was there was for the people in charge of the cell within the cell. I t was a well organized small community.

"Unless water is coming out of the tap inside the cell, all of these people cannot bath." One of my friend Burundian but entered Zambia as a Congolese who was crossing Zambia toward South Africa the land of the late Nelson Mandela, gave me the condition for me to take bath. He was there for two months.

I prayed: "Lord, I want to take bath, please let the water comes through the tap so that I can bath and Lord, change the climate; Remove hotness in the cell for all the time I will be the cell!"

At my surprise, In the evening, it rained (it was a rainy season but the day I visited the cell it was not raining for some days. The sun was hitting seriously Lusaka the capital of the great Christian nation of Zambia).

It rained and the water came out of the tap. All the prisoners went to take bath one by one! I was happy for the answer to my prayer that was benefiting other people as well. They were blessed through me.

God is faithful wherever you are. His promises are yes and amen through Christ. I love the way our beloved Jesus Christ the God of gods and Lord of lords He is faithful. I love righteousness.

Can I tell you that the hotness disappeared from that day up to the day I left the cell on the fifth day? Our God is awesome! The night before the fifth day which was the last day in the cell, I was reading Psalm71:3"… **give the command to save me, for you are my rock and my fortress**." Then I heard the Holy Spirit telling me:"give a command yourself to come out of the cell!" I then commanded in the name of Jesus as I was told.

You can't believe that early in the morning of the fifth day of my visitation in that dark "world", I heard people calling me:'' Burundian wake up you are called by an immigration officer!"

I was released without going in the court and a policeman asked me:"How come you are released without going in the court?"; others left the place with handcuffs but me nothing was on my hands and left the cell as a free man back to town with a new visa without paying any money according to my prayer to my beloved God in whom I trust. People in the cell, Zambians were happy I was released. They loved me and I loved them and prayed for them. All human beings we are here on earth to love each other and be united as one people against our common enemies:" famine, diseases, climate,…"

In the same night I talked to my people in the cell when they asked me to lead them in prayer. The Holy Spirit pushed me to prophecy over them:**'Tomorrow some of you are going to be released!"**

The day I was made free the following day of that declaration which was the day I was also released there 2 young men who were released miraculously and they praised God and told me:" **God is big!**", "**yes He is**". I agreed with them!

Maybe I was sent in the cell for them and for the release of all so called foreigners that I found there because none of them remained there! I like to see people are happy; I love the people, the sheep of God!

Jesus said to Peter if you love me take care of my sheep! A leader is called to feed spiritually and physically and protect the sheep. And one way to feed the people is to create jobs for the sheep. This is kind of a leader in order of Melchizedek, the righteous king of peace.

Leaders (presidents, kings, governors,…) from all over the World make sure you are taking care of the people of Christ, his people wholeheartedly, cheerfully and loving them with all your hearts, strength, soul,) as your own family! Do not sleep and be comfortable when some of your people are in the street, you are fathers of fatherless and fight for widows and foreigners. God says:" **Any immigrant who lives with you must be treated as if they were one of your citizens. You must love them as yourself, because you were immigrants in the land of Egypt; I am the LORD your God.**" Leviticus 19:34, Common English Bible

Don't be comfortable when some of your people are homeless while you are enjoying nice beds! Take care of the so called foreigners whether legal or illegal, love them as your own people and instead of rushing into deportation integrate them in the society! If some of them you are calling them "dreamers" if you take care of them as your own people, your own children; they may dream bigger than your! Just create an environment that will help them to dream big! You will never go wrong by doing like that. Love and mercy will produce in abundance love and mercy!

Are you seeing why I have vowed to my God that once the king of the entire World, I will make sure the whole World is practicing the righteousness of God? It is because I love the people and only the righteousness of our Lord Jesus Christ will benefit the people, it will protect them, there will be no diseases and people will live long, peacefully, prosperous. "It is written:" **If and you shall serve the Lord your God, and he shall bless thy bread, and thy water; and I will take sickness away from the midst of thee. There shall nothing cast their young, nor be barren, in thy land: the number of thy days I will fulfill." Exodus 23:25-26**. Remember that Jesus is the same yesterday, today and forever!

I praise my heavenly father for have put climate in my hands in the name of Jesus. The key of David was working perfectly against the weather: **"To open and no one can shut, to shut and no one can open."**

I praise also my savior and my rock Jesus Christ for remembering my righteousness and saved from the hands of the chief immigration officer who escorted me when I was released. Was he apologizing? I don't know but we separate peacefully and I told him: "Thank you and God bless you!"

GOD ALWAYS STANDS MIGHTLY FOR THOSE WHO CHOOSE CHEERFULLY TO STAND FOR HIS WAYS!

I realized that the Lord had given me the power over the climate. When others fear the climate change I do not have fear why? It is the climate to fear me because the creator of the climate has given me power over it! Thank you Jesus Christ for dying for the sin of the World and now I have access to the promises of God including the key of David. The Lord gives the key of David to guide like a shepherd leading his sheep, his people in the ways of righteousness because He loves his people. It is written that God punishes those he loves!

Do you want to hear again how doing what is right according to God is important to your life? There is always a reward to whoever chooses to do what is right with God liking doing good to people. I can give you another example of my Aunt... She had hepatitis C and she was told that there was a new medicine: Harvoni which was a new hepatitis C medication combining Sofosbuvir and LedipasvirLedispavir which provides nearly 100 percent per cent cure.

What the challenge! In all Africa that medicine was not found anywhere even in South Africa at that time. Her son got someone from USA who promised to give up to $200.000 to pay for all the treatment process.

The challenge was to be in the country where they can provide with the medicine. She tried to look for a US visa but in vain. She told a former vice president in Burundi:" Please save a life and help me and put me in the list of journalists who follow you if you go in a country where I can get the treatment."

What did the vice president respond?

Let first you daughter be a member of our political party and then we will help you! We refused the offer we said: "The Lord will make a way without him!"

She went to talk to her boss at her workplace as journalist for the government was the director to help her to get a mission. My Aunt is a fighter; she is a woman of faith! But even the boss refused to help her! I asked her:" why not go to any embassy and tell them you want to go where the medicine can be administrated?" She answered me that if she said so they will not give her visa she needed.

What happened later? I remembered what my Aunt did for my late beloved mother who was a close friend of mine, a powerful mother who would encourage me during my medical studies, who raised me in the ways of God! My Aunt paid the treatment fees in an expensive hospital right in Bujumbura the capital of Burundi.

"My God help me to save the life of this great woman Aunt who tried to save my mother!" I asked my God to use and be her source of blessing the same way she blessed my mother. The good works will push people to support you! They have power over and can speak for you! Therefore love to do good!

I started telling her every evening: "Congratulation Aunt!"

"For what?" She would ask me. "Eh! I am told you have a visa!" I would answer her. And she would tell me you are right by faith I have the visa! We would laugh but being sure that faith does work! You know what when you walking by faith according to the will of God something can happen anytime. You have to be ready for the answer from God.

One day there I was invited to participate in a medical meeting in Germany this great nation whose chief of the government is a great woman that I respect as my mother who loves her people Angel Merkel. I learnt from my own late mother to consider some women as my mother as a respect to them because they deserve it.

I took that opportunity to send my Aunt in Germany. Finally she got a visa but her worry was that in Germany there were not a lot of Burundians like in Belgium. She was advised to go in Belgium. But I told her remember what we told those who invite you as journalist that you will attend the meeting:

"Please do what we promised them and you will see what God can do to whoever keeps words at all cost! I believe and I have seen that faithfulness pays back! I told her if you choose faithfulness and follow what I am telling you will see the hand of God! I and her husband who is also a great man of faith chose to rely on God and his righteousness. I love The US president His keeping his promises to his great and beloved people of America.

I knew that if my dear Aunt chose to go in Germany according to what we promised to those who invited her; God would make Germany love her! The bible says that "To the faithful, God shows himself as faithful".

Some people told her Germany do not love black people but I said it is a lie! I believe if you love a people, the people will love you back. If you bless someone you will receive blessing back no matter what! Righteousness will always profit you! The easier way to receive blessing even more than what you want it is to bless others first.

His majesty King of kings Jesus Christ said: "Do to others whatever you would like them to do to you. This is the essence of all that is taught in the law and the prophets." **Matthew 7:12, New Living Translation**.

I thank God that she definitely attended the meeting and she was happy. Do you know who took care of her? God had prepared an angel to her, a great woman white national of Germany older than her to take care of my Aunt! She helped her before she started treatment! Her medical doctor in Germany was a good man, a good doctor who tried to do whatever he can to help her get the treatment. Finally the government of Germany paid for her all treatment till she was healed!

God bless all my beloved great people of Germany! May prosperity and righteousness of God be your potion!

On the December 28th 2018, while I was in the presence of the Ancient of days our beloved Go and Savior I prayed writing from my praying room:"

Holy Father, good, and Almighty God if you fulfill your Word to me and become a king with great power over all the earth in your name as one kingdom ,one nation, one family; and be like their respected loved father with the wisdom that beat the one you give Solomon for me to take care well your people father and make richer than Solomon with wealth in trillions of US dollars to remove the shame that King Solomon who is better than Solomon and may always remain loyal to you, may you protect me from the sin our forefather David never reign over me;

Then:

1. **I will destroy all idols from all over the World and your name Lord Jesus will be only name that will be worshipped as God, so that the whole world be fill with your knowledge and your glory**

2.   I will hate what you hate and as your holy Spirit will guide me I will set up your laws as our laws in all your my kingdom which is your kingdom;

3.   I will change the names of planet that are called according to the name of idols to purify heavens;

4.   Every day I will spend one hour bowing down in worship as a sacrifice of thanksgiving for the having found favor before you my God, my father and the rock of my salvation to choke the Devil who wanted you to bow down and worship him;

5.   At the palace we will be praising you every Wednesday ;

6.   I will deliver the needy when he cries; the poor also; and the one does not have no helper. I will spare their poor and the needy, and I will save the lives of the needy. I will redeem their life from the deceit and violence: and their blood will be precious in my sight.

7.   I will judge your people with righteousness and save the children of the needy, and I will break in pieces the oppressor

8.   May I be as the my people which is your people Oh Lord as the light of the morning, when the sunrises, even a morning without clouds; as the tender grass springing out of the earth by clear shining after rain;

9.   Let me my Lord God and Father come down like rain upon the mown grass: as showers that water the earth;

10. Let oh God in my days the righteous flourish and abundance of peace so long as the moon endures.

11. And because will be filled with your righteousness and your justice, then let peace overshadow the earth and prosperity all over the earth.

12. May you protect my health for the sake of your name and give me extraordinary to be able to take care of your people properly

13. Guide me oh Lord how to structure worship in all your kingdom like what king David did in his time

14. May the people say: Blessed is the king who comes in the name of Jesus Christ; blessed be the coming of our father David!

MY BELOVED PEOPLE FROM ALL OVER THE WORLD LOVE RIGHTEOUSNESS OF GOD WITH ALL YOUR HEART BEFORE THE LORD JESUS CHRIST PUNISH YOU TO TEACH YOU TO HONOR HIS NAME!

Let me show two other examples of doing what is right saving a life.

Can I tell you something? One day I saved a baby whose the mother was determined to destroy a nation that was in her womb!

She was a lady about 20 years old. She came in our medical office and said:" Doctor, can you help me? I am pregnant, I am still a student, my boyfriend insists to put an end to his pregnancy. I tried to use contraception method but in vain. The reason I want to abort also is that at my school will no longer allow me to study with my pregnancy!"

The blood of rejected people will be my interest like these innocent great and strong nations in the womb of their mother favored by God to carry in them nations but despise their mission in the World.

"Do you know how many would like to conceive but they cannot?"

That is what I utilized to convince that young lady who came in our medical office. She wanted us to help her to abort. As I have already told you she tried to give us all reasons. She used contraception method in vain.

It was not the first time using contraception method. She had sexual relations which normally end up to a pregnancy because God instituted that to multiply mankind.

When you are involved in such relations be assured what you are dealing with. And because people want to be clever than their creature they use contraception to avoid pregnancy. They choose to commit adultery and fortification (sexual act outside marriage) and try to avoid the outcome: "The conception of a baby."

My young patient succeeded to kill some eggs but there an egg that tried to fight back, maybe God gave it strength, The egg was a champion who managed to overcome the contraception method.

The fetus grew up secretly in the Womb and provoked some changes in the life of her beloved mother. The heart of that wonderful baby was beating "illegally" in the house where it invaded against the will of the mother.

It was called "unintended" pregnancy. Thank God the owner of the "producing system" was willing to develop the baby against the will of the servant, the mother who was not consulted because she was just a vessel to people the World.

When Jesus was about to come in the world an angel of God Gabriel informed marry and told him:" You are highly favored!" Beloved women from all over the World you should be thankful to God who entrusted you with wombs so that God might renew the strength of the World by bringing news persons in the world! You should not fight against your creator!

"Is the heart beating?" The mother asked us pointing at the scan.

"Yes, it is." My friend replied him.

"Why not give chance to your baby to enjoy life like you? Do you know what kind of a baby you have? Do you know what your baby is going to be in the world in case you give a chance for the baby to survive?" I tried to fight for the baby convincing the mother to keep her fruit!

 I gave her a story of a woman who had children and was trying natural family planning. She wanted to stop giving birth to the new strength of the World, to the future of the World because children are a future for the World.

It is God who chooses who to people the Earth according to his plan He has before the foundation of the universe. God is in charge of what is happening around the whole Universe more than what you thing. There is no reason you can abort even after rape.

When that lady who had already 5 children found herself pregnant, she was not happy. She went to a certain hospital to see a doctor to help her abort. On the Queue waiting to see the doctor, she heard another woman saying that she came to see the doctor because she wanted children. She wanted to become pregnant and have children. She came to the doctor to help her become a mother like other women.

When that lady realized that there is someone who had come because she wanted to conceive, she was chocked and said in her heart: "I want to abort while there is someone who is struggling to conceive?" Immediately she changed her mind and went back home fully decided to keep the baby.

I continued to tell my patient how that baby who was a girl became a good source of happiness to her mother and the father. She is very intelligence loyal to the parents. She is done with university. She loves God.

"You see, there are many women who want just to conceive like you but it is not possible for them. Please keep your baby and love the baby with all your heart and God will bless you! Your baby may be a great solution to the World! If you think your boyfriend can leave you because you have decided to keep the baby; God will give you a better boyfriend who liked the way you decided to save the baby." I gave her finally a last word to choose to keep the baby or not.

"I will keep my baby! Thank you doctor." She decided to keep the baby. I was very happy that I helped the baby to survive a potential rejection. That day I praise my beloved God the great father of the mankind for making a medical doctor. Hallelujah!

"The stone that builders rejected has become a cornerstone." Cornerstone always experiences rejection from builders". Beloved America, Europe, Australia… those people so called foreigners whether "legal or illegal" you want to deport (to abort and vomit from you) are maybe the new strength you want. They are maybe cornerstones you need for your greatness. Give them a chance and you will see!

"If you save the life, God will save your life also but if you do not you will regret all your life because a human being was crying to you and you refuse to help. I did not want my patient to behave like those people from my great and beloved people of France who refused to save the lives of their friends and brothers Tutsi who were fleeing their own brothers who were looking to kill them in Rwanda.

Thank God now my beloved and great people of France they cannot sit and watch what is happening in the World. They helped in Ivory coast, Mali… That is what the World needs now.

A people that help each other because if you are fighting for the security of others you are making yourself safer and secure somehow. I congratulate the people of France, America and all nations that involve themselves saving other people from other nations. When you are doing like that you are defending your interest somehow as well.

I thank God for the development in my beloved and great people of China and I think they are able to help other nations to experience their own development effectively. If you make other nations great it is like you are helping yourself. To save their economy is another way of saving the life of people! It is good to save lives and protect them from death or disaster.

Speak out for the needy and helpless! Prevent loss of life at any cost!

I am grateful to God who helped me to try to save a life of a man who was Hutu in Burundi:

"When the late great president Ndadaye Melchior (He was the first democratically elected and first Hutu president of Burundi after winning the landmark 1993 election. May his soul rest in peace!) who beat his opponents in Burundi was killed 3 months later after winning the election; some people from this great family of Hutu in Burundi killed their friends, brothers from the great family of Tutsi to avenge courageous the president Ndadaye Melchior who was Hutu.

When some of Tutsi people who were in the capital of Bujumbura began to kill their brothers Hutu to avenge theirs, I was in Musaga where I was born.

 I was in the primary school in the sixth year. I started seeing innocent people killed live like you are watching a movie. Their brothers who were supposed to save them killed those using stones, some sticks called in Kirundi the Burundian local language "Umuganuro". I was a boy and I couldn't believe what I was observing.

I was taught to know who is Tutsi or Hutu. Even before the victory of Ndadaye Melchior some of my friends of my neighbors, children with whom I would spend time together started calling me with a strange bad view a "Tutsi".

They were already taught by their parents while children My father and my mother never taught us hatred. They have never taught me that I am different from my friends. They knew I am human being and I should love other human being like me without any division. They taught me love of Christ Jesus to everyone. I grew up with that mentality.

I would make friends from all tribes. Hutu or Tutsi, people so called foreigners whether "legal" or "illegal". As long as they are human beings like me then they are legal because we have the same source. They have right to be loved by me and me by them. Our source- Jesus Christ-commanded us to love each other! We are condemned to save each other.

It is not a crime to be called Tutsi or Hutu what is bad is to use that as a reason to destroy someone's life! One should be proud who he is. I thank God he chose for me to come in the World as so called ''Tutsi'' the same way I thank God He chose for me to be born in Burundi, in Africa as a black who found himself in the same world where God put me people who are white but human beings like me, and I thank God for everyone in the World. I need them and they need me as well.

I am a medical doctor and others are farmers for instance. We need each other. There is a reason why God created people in different aspects. I think the same way me as a medical doctor I need a farmer in the same way a Hutu needs a Tutsi. A black needs a white person and vice versa.

God commanded human beings to not commit murders? Maybe it is because the one you want to kill has gifts you do not have and therefore you need them for your existence! I realized that all laws that God gave the world like "do not commit murder" are for our good!

So in Musaga, a certain evening I saw that human being like me who was Hutu, a good guy, brown, older than me who was in that area in the wrong time.

When I met him when I was going to get something a bit far from our home, I told him:" please leave this place because I am hearing (my father commanded us to remain home). He was protecting us from seeing what was happening!) That people like you are being killed. I do know if he managed to live but I did my job: "saving and preventing a loss of a life!"

My dream is to see people loving each other and reject any hatred. I have given myself to the Lord Jesus Christ like David king over the Whole World, their beloved shepherd who takes care of them with love, humility and respect.

Another thing we should do as leaders is to save lives by protecting our people from anything that can harm them. How many people are dying because of drinking and smoking? It is not enough to say that tobacco can harm because people will still smoke or drink. The best way to protect then is to ban those products among us. How much money are we spending publicly because of that?

If one is drinking and becomes drunk and commit a crime. Who is responsible? The one who is drunk becomes so because he found easily the drink that means even the seller is responsible; and the main responsible is the government who allow those alcoholic drinks to be sold easily.

The drunkard is dependant he is condemned to drink. He was not born drinking there is a beginning because it easy to find such a destructive drink on the market. If he commit a crime and you put him in jail you are also destroying the whole family if he is a father.

The best way to protect the people is to put away anything that can take them to destruction directly or indirectly instead of building prisons for them yet it is the government that made access easily to the poison that caused all the damage.

We all know how dangerous it is to smoke tobacco but instead of removing that poison from the people we teach them how dangerous it is! Those who are smoking are already dependant they do not care as long as the poison is available. Why not remove that poison among my people?

I was reading about the nations that do not allow alcoholic drink and tobacco how the death toll due to those poisons is almost null in comparison of the nations that allow them.

In Zambia, a nation declared in the constitution a "Christian nation" people drink and some of them are dying, others do not care about their future.

One lady told:"Dr, my son is 40 years old but he drinks a lot, he does not think about his future. He is divorced because of his drinking behavior. Drinking is destroying families, nations.

Zambia wake up and stop that. The devil is laughing at you! Nations that are not declared Christian nation are not drinking you should be wiser than them. But I am glad that I heard that now Zambia is against the some drinks that are destroying our beloved young men and women.

Beloved great president Lungu, I really appreciate what you declared the October 18th of every year as a "national prayer day". God bless you for that! Let Zambia live, work; think properly because nothing is disturbing their mind! Let my people be wise! I know you love our great people of Zambia!

 Dear great and beloved president Putin protects my beloved people of Russia from perishing because of drinking! Make Russia wise again!

Protect my people from destroying themselves!

How many are dying in America because of smoking? How much the government is losing because of that! Make America wise again!

LEADERS FROM ALL OVER THE WORLD PLEASE DO NOT HELP MY BELOVED PEOPLE TO DESTROY THEMSELVES AND MAKE OUR WORLD SAFE AND PURELY GREAT! IF YOU DO NOT DO THAT THEIR BLOOD ARE ON YOUR HANDS BECAUSE GOD GAVE YOU AUTHORITY TO PROTECT HIS SHEEP!

Chapter 4. What men of God said about directly or not.

In 2017 I was in a church (**Jesus Anointed Ministries International**) whose overseer is a courageous and full of faith man of God; a great man that I love called Bishop **Billy Mfula** (a man who is wise and like wisdom, humble, who fought one day as a courageous young person but full of the love for Christ; when some people wanted to remove the declaration of Zambia as a Christian nation from the constitution) in Lusaka during lunch time, a man of God **Henry**

Danso from Ghana called me from where I was seated in the public and declared to the church:" Watch out to this man in two years!"

Immediately I remembered what I asked some 2 or 3 days ago to the Lord in prayer. The question to my God was "When I am going to impact the world?"Am I going to start impacting the world in 2 years? In 2019? I did not understand what he was saying but I kept that in my heart. Nothing happen by accident in this world!

So, when the year of 2019 was about to be reached, toward the last months I started saying:" **My time of impacting nations has come**!" I started telling the Lord to make people trust in me or to reveal what is going to happen in future like what He did in the time of Moses and David and the Lord did it as you are going to see that in the following points:

1. The Lord announced to the world through Dr David oyedebo what He is going to do according to the mission He has put on my heart.

During Shiloh 2018 December 4th 2018 * 7Pm: Shiloh Opening Session (Shiloh is a church programme organized by the Living Faith Church International A.K.A Winners Chapel. It is a yearly programme which takes about one week at Faith Tabernacle, Canaan land, Ota.) in Nigeria in the month of December 2018, a powerful man of God well known internationally , Dr David Oyedebo, the presiding Bishop of the Living Faith Church Worldwide a.k.a Winners' Chapel, said:

"This is a dominion era of the church. *The time of the holy people of the Most High has com according to the book of Daniel 7:27 Amplified Bible version:* "Then the kingdom and the dominion and the greatness of all the kingdoms under the whole heaven will be given to the people of the saints (believers) of the Most High; His kingdom will be an everlasting kingdom, and all the dominions will serve and obey Him.".

Authority shall be domiciled in the church of the last days. It is a divine agenda. Be sensitive to the God timing.

The salvation is universal it is for all nations according to Revelation5:10. The Authority that enthrones us is from heaven. God has come down to manifest himself among his people. It is a time of glorification of his church.

"This is the plan determined for the whole world; this is the hand stretched out over all nations. For the Lord Almighty has purposed, and who can thwart him? His hand is stretched out, and who can turn it back?" Isaiah 14Isaiah14:26-27, New International Version."

I have never talked to the man of God Dr David Oyedebo. The Lord Jesus Christ chose him to announce to all the earth what He is going to do via his David who has come in the name of Jesus Christ. It is me working together through prayers with the believers of Christ Jesus the God of all the earth. And because I have come in the name of Jesus Christ whoever is against me is against Jesus Christ himself but whoever will support will be loved by God the Father, Jesus Christ and the Holy Spirit. I wonder how the enemy can win against the one who created Him Jesus Christ the creator of Heavens and the earth.

I would like to remind you what happened to Saul before he became Apostle Paul to prove to you that when you work with the Lord Jesus whoever touches you is doing it against Jesus Christ Himself. Saul was busy persecuting the disciples of Jesus Christ.

He was going to Damascus to catch disciples or Christians and Jesus stopped and changed him into another man :

"As he neared Damascus on his journey, suddenly a light from heaven flashed around him. He fell to the ground and heard a voice say to him, "Saul, Saul, why do you persecute me?"

[5] **"Who are you, Lord?" Saul asked.**

"I am Jesus, whom you are persecuting," he replied. [6] **"Now get up and go into the city, and you will be told what you must do."** Actes9; 3-6, New International Version.

Can I continue without writing this verse in Daniel4:17;"This is the decision of the alert and watchful angels. So then, let all people everywhere know that the Supreme God has power over human kingdoms and that he can give them to anyone he chooses--even to those who are least important."' GOOD NEWS TRANSLATION version.

2. Before the end year of 2018 in a certain Sunday of December, I was in church of a man I love also called Prophet Elvis Muzanga, a man of God overseeing "**Power life Embassy ministry**" in Zambia, Lusaka. I have never talked to this man. What he knows about me I am a medical

doctor. He said loudly in front of us in the church: "Something is going to happen in 2019. Someone is going to operate on an international platform. Something big is going to happen." And He asked the church: "Do you see what I am seeing?"

I cried in agreeing with him and said:"Yes, it is true." Like marry the mother to Jesus, I kept that also in my heart.

Remember, In Psalm89:27 the Lord Jesus Christ has promised to make him His firstborn (preeminent), the highest of the kings of the earth." In order words, a ruler, or a leader of leaders. This is to work on international platform in any way.

3. How God confirmed my role as a leader of leaders through a woman of God from USA!

I started posting some messages on my facebook toward the end of 2018 in line of my divine vision about leading the whole world always remembering what the man of God Henry Danso said about me in the church in 2017:"**Watch out this man in 2 years!**"

I started seeing the entire world as my nation, my people. I started praying for all nations, following what is happening around the globe. So in December 07, 2018 I posted a message on my facebook timeline just to fight in prayer for my beloved and great people of Yemen and said:"

*A   new   WORLD   ORDER:
One   World   Kingdom   one   Nation   under   one   God   Jesus   Christ   the   King   of   kings!*

My beloved people of the World, We must stop immediately this war between our beloved people of Yemen. We cannot continue looking to a staving Yemenite people while the whole world is watching like what happened in Rwanda in 1994 when two brave people that needed each other Tutsi and Hutu killed each other while the world was watching.

The World woke up after genocide of Tutsi was already committed and we the people of the world have created a criminal tribunal for those who were involved in genocide instead of preventing that genocide.

Those who were killed during that period Tutsi or Hutu were A big loss not only to Rwanda or Africa, but it was a loss of the whole World! Enough is enough! We must stop equally immediately the war between our beloved people of Syria and between our two brave, brothers and great peoples Israel and Palestine. Our dearest planet cannot be great if our own people in Afghanistan, Pakistan, and some African countries are not peaceful. Something must be done. We have to put aside selfishness and we the people save one another at all cost! The World is like a human body and if one organ is not performing well then the whole body cannot function properly. Sometimes we have to use the word ''disable'' to a person whose one part or more is not okay. Likewise, all the nations of our World; the planet Earth form one body. If one nation is not okay, then the whole World is not okay. If Yemen is not okay for example, then we have a ''disable'' World. The World cannot be great at all! Nowadays the World is like a small village, it is no longer a time of working alone. The season cannot allow you it anymore! The time of isolationism is over! If we want a great world, we should not work as G20 only when God made sure that the World should work together as one family. That is why you find some materials we need for our industries are found for example in Zambia(copper, gold,…), in Congo(where USUSA got from the uranium used for the atomic bomb during the second world war),in South Arabia for the petrol,…

There is not a nation, an ethnicity, a race… that is not useful for the greatness of our world. We need a G World instead of G20! Every part of our body is useful for the proper functioning of our body. The hands have their role; the legs have theirs, etc. The Creator of our brain has created white people because black people need them, and vice versa.

He created Chinese because Americans need them and vice versa. He created Palestinians because the Israelis need them and vice versa. North Koreans need southerners and vice versa. He created Bemba because the Lozi (Tribes in Zambia) need them and vice versa, He created Tutsi because the Hutu(tribes in Rwanda and in Burundi) need them and vice versa, Our Creator is extremely smarter than us humans beings. You cannot say that you are independent of others to be great. Our dear heavenly Father put some of the ingredients you need for your assignment in someone else. We need each other we all interdependent, interconnected! The American soil was unknown to the world before other peoples of the world come to go there. And now it's the first world power. The American soil has understood that its greatness is hiding in other peoples of the world and it is because of it continues to attract other peoples like these good people along the Mexico-USA border. It's as if the American soil is shouting " remove this wall of separation; I need this people to keep growing up. "

Our beloved people of China began to be more prosperous when it opened to the world. This is not the moment of Brexit; true prosperity is really possible in the union with the other members of our "body", our whole World.

The United States became a superpower in the 50 states that united in one nation under one leader

We can form a more prosperous world, a world of peace, a very secure world (because we are going to destroy our weapons of mass destruction like atomic bombs and put forward the massive construction weapon that is love) and more about if we put together all the peoples of the whole world as one nation, one family, with English as an official language, under one Chief;

A whole world (including those who live in the forests as they are also our people.) In one nation, one kingdom under one King of the Kings Jesus Christ as our God and Savior. Our dearest Jesus Christ died so that the whole world may be God's people of Abraham, Isaac and Jacob, not just our dear great people of Israel. And for that He poured out his own blood to take away the sin of the world. His love is indescribable and it is very wise to declare: " Lord God and Savior Jesus Christ, we are one world kingdom under your laws because you are our LORD OF THE LORDS and OUR KING OF KINGS. The MESSIAHMESSAIH.

Our great beloved people of Zambia had decided wisely to declare Jesus Christ the Lord and the king of Zambia when we declared Zambia a ''Christian nation''. There is no wisdom that can beat that one.

Americans, Africans, Europeans, Asians, Oceanic... we are all one people under one God and FATHER!

''But now, O LORD, thou art our father; we are the clay, and thou our potter; and we all are the work of thy hand.'' Isaiah 64:8, KJV.

"Let all the earth fear the LORD; let all the people of the world revere him."psalm33:8;

"For all the gods of the peoples are worthless idols, but the LORD made the heavens."psalm96:5;

Isaiah 9:6 "For to us a child is born, to us a son is given, and the government will be on his shoulders. And He will be called Wonderful Counselor, Mighty God, Everlasting Father, and Prince of Peace."

Do you want to discover a powerful comment from a powerful woman of God from my beloved great nation United State of America? She is a prophetess called **Judith Peart** I did know her before she commented on the post. She is one of my facebook friends.

She said commenting on the above post:" That is powerful.

· You should publish this.

Contact my husband Donald Peart he can help you get published.

Prepare a manuscript. God is going to launch your ministry. You are called to be a voice to the places unheard and places people refuse to see. You will be a fresh bold voice in this time. You have not yet seen the things God will do. And she continued:"

I hear the Lord say ...my son no longer will you be comfortable. Stretch out your rod. The power is in you. The nations will hear your voice. Arise oh son of mine.

Do what you think can't be done. You are a leader to leaders. Your voice will be heard to those in high places. Make yourself new, refresh yourself, prepare yourself. You will be known as he who speaks truth. A light I give you. Take that light to the world. They may reject you. But know they rejected me.

There are those who will hear your voice. My voice in you. Be a trumpet to my people. Be a voice of conscience of reason to those who know me not. Awake oh man of God. Awake to your season. I will connect you to those around you who will pour into you. I will call the resources from the earth to help you. Stand firm. Be unmovable. Today you have been stirred to arise. Don't delay. Don't look at your ability. Know that it is me in you.

Prophetess **Judith** **Peart**

Crown of Glory Ministries Md. "

She said about a manuscript and I was going to start writing a book on my world vision. I promised her that I was going to write the book.

Guess what? I started writing the book. I would save the files titled "The powerful book that is about to shake the world!"

Then One day I prayed to the Lord:" **My God, I would like a man of God who is white because my assignment is for all people from different races confirming what is about to happen through me.**

I do not like to be in a box of black people only although I am proud I am black because my God chose it for me for a reason of my creator but I want to connect to every human being that God created .Everyone in the world is my neighbor and I love them. I remember telling my God *:"Lord you have been using black men of God, can use a white man of God of yours to prophesy over me about what you are going to do by my hands?"* The following is the answer that shows how God used His servant Dr **Israel Ashley McguickenMc Guicken**.

4. Another proof from a great man of God Dr Israel Ashley McguickenMc Guicken

Some days later A powerful man of God from United State of America California **Dr Israel Ashley McguickenMc Guicken** came in our church in Zambia and prophesied to the congregation that "**someone is going to shake the world. He is a great leader**." After he left Zambia I talked to him about the prophecy that it was about me through facebook(May God bless those who created this international platform).

He was very happy for the testimony. I told him about the book and asked if he can allow me to mention his name in my book and he agreed to it. He is a good man and humble and great man of God. And he added:" **exciting time!**"

5. Another proof from a very friend of mine man of God Bishop Billy Mfula

Before the end of the year of 2018 in the last days of December, I was in a church. I heard a voice telling me that I should talk to a man of God Called Bishop Billy Mfula to pray for me according to my assignment. I said:" **Lord, Remember that I talked to him about my vision**

when I told him that I have asked God to make me the Leader of all nations united in one nation. So Lord, if this voice is from you, tell him yourself to pray for me."

I was surprised when the man of God Bishop Billy Mfula said after eating what he called "a prophetic meal at his place":" **This meal is to cerebrate your assignment."** He said boldly.

:" **Thank you and God bless you!"** I replied to Him.

He also pray and say:" **The Heaven has released you; therefore the earth cannot stop you from doing your assignment!"**

I praised the Lord my God who trusted in me for that powerful confirmation that He is with me. I did not talk to Bishop Billy Mfula but God did it for me. When we speak to God who created our ears do hear and answer our prayers!

He is really our everlasting Good heavenly Father! Hallelujah! I praise him and thank him for his favor toward me his humble son who has given himself to Him to be used like King David in this last day!

The powerful woman of God Prophetess Judith Peart spoke about rejection toward me that is true because God cannot tell you that He is will crush my foes and plague those who hate me without himself seeing adversaries.

God is faithful and He sees what is before us. I prayed and fasted 7 days before the end of 2018. I was praying for the year of 2019 and my vision for the Lord to strengthen me for his Kingdom.

The   Holy   Spirit   told   me:" **So   do   not   fear,   for   I   am   with   you;   do   not   be   dismayed,   for   I   am   your   God.**

I will strengthen you and help you;

I will uphold you with my righteous right hand.

[11] **"All who rage against you will surely be ashamed and disgraced; those who oppose you will be as nothing and perish.** [12] **Though you search for your enemies, you will not find them. Those who wage war against you will be as nothing at all.** [13] **For I am the Lord your God who takes hold of your right hand and says to you, Do not fear;**

I will help you." Isaiah 41Isaiah41:10-13, New International Version (NIV).

Through these divine words I can say that I am under a divine protection. The Lord himself is my shield. I am untouchable! Hallelujah and Glory to my Rock of my salvation, Jesus Christ!

A king can be saved and win because of God through His Word. Moses won against Pharaoh through the Word of God in his mouth without a strong army because God can do everything using His power according to His will.

I am very grateful for the God my heavenly father who has removed from me fear of a man. How? You can see it yourself through this following Example:"

There is a day I cannot forget in my life. I was coming from town from where I was working from as a medical doctor. It was night back home in Jabe a city that is in town.

"Doctor, why are you coming here? All the young men have left Jabe because General Adolf Nshimirimana is coming tonight to kill people who protested against the president Nkurunziza Peter." My beloved cousin told me back home. I think it was around 8hours PM.

The city of Jabe has a lot of people who did not want to see the president Nkurunziza Peter to stand for the third term as a Burundian president. General Adolf Nshimirimana was a tall man, courageous, a very friend to his excellence President Nkurunziza.

General Adolf was much feared in the opposition camp. Previously we were told although I am not sure if it is true but people were saying that he is the one who had killed people in the opposition camp in other town of Bujumbura called "Mutakura" where a man (according to some news) was killed with everyone who was in his house despite him being on his knees before the late General Adolphe Nshimirimana begging General Adolf not to kill him.

I was told that General Adolf was furious that day because of some people in that area of Mutakura tried to assassinate him but failed.

Mutakura was one of the areas in the capital of Bujumbura that protested against the president Nkurunziza Peter including Jabe where I was staying.

I think that he late General Nshimirimana behaved in the same way like what happened in Burundi when in 1972 a Hutu rebel faction tried to overthrow the Tutsi ruler Micombero Michel who was the president after deposing the King Ntare V.

A systematic massacre followed against Hutu leaders and university students. Half of the country's eight thousand Hutu teachers were eliminated. Over a third of three hundred thirty teacher- training students died. Burundi has a dark history of blood.

I never participated in the demonstration but where I was staying they did with all their strength. So to hear that General Adolf was coming in our area of Jabe whether that was true or not it was a good information enough to create fear in me.

I started shaking all my body. I do not remember if I manage to have enough appetite for my super. In that night on my bed I remember the word of God that says:" **I, even I, am He who comforts you. Who are you that you are afraid of a man who dies? Why are you afraid of the sons of men who are made like grass, that you have forgotten the Lord who made you? He spread out the heavens and put the earth in its place. Why do you live in fear all day long because of the anger of the one who makes it hard for you as he makes ready to destroy? But where is his anger?" Isaiah 51:12-13, New Life Version.**

I started confessing the Word of God saying I refuse to fear a man who can die. I refused to neglect the information and prayed: "Lord if it is true General Adolf is coming; you can stop him from coming."

I would see myself being killed among others but I would reject that vision but confess that I refuse to fear a man who dies. I chose to let the Word of God prevail in my heart. It was a tough spiritual warfare.

I manage to sleep in peace because of the Word of God that the Holy Spirit put in my heart to help me remain peaceful. I wake up in morning and nothing happened that night. Was it a lie or God who stopped him from coming in our area of Jabe? I do not know.

You know what? Some days later on a certain Sunday I heard that General Adolf Nshimirimana is no longer among the living human beings.

He was killed by people I do not know. I kept hearing some questions in my spirit:" Why did you fear a dying man? Where is he now? There is a fear that can beat you when you have committed a sin but when you are right with God you do not have a right of fearing a man who dies. That is how God removed forever the fear of man. **The LORD is with me; I will not be afraid. What can mere mortals do to me?" Psalm 118:6, New International Version.**

Chapter 5: Rule nations to fulfill the great commission easily

Our Lord Jesus Christ is the king of kings. He died for our sins that were against Him and his laws so that we can be able to imitate him as a good leader, a good ruler, a good shepherd, in short a good God fearing politician children of God

Our Lord Jesus is expecting us to be the light of the World as a city on a hill that cannot be hidden and as the salt of the World. Therefore Christians -worshippers in true and in spirit- you should not hide yourself but you should be available to bring light in the world. What is the light of God? You may ask. Isn't? The light of God is His laws. Without the commandments of our God the world is lost.

Jesus refused to be directly a king to his people because. He knew that he came on the Earth to produce kings of his kind to rule on the Earth in his name according to his will, to his laws which are the light of the World! He says my Kingdom is not of this world.

God put you on the highest mountain in your country to see where your people can not see to provide them what they need. At the top of your people, you can see where they cannot see. You have in your hands right to set up laws for your interest and their interest and not only for your own interest.

The will of our beloved Lord Jesus Christ who loves us till to his death at the cross is to see the whole world governed according to His laws. You know what? When you are a leader of the people your job it is to discipline your people in the same way you discipline your children for their good. So as a leader it is your duty to know exactly what it is good for yourself and for your people.

When Jesus taught us how to pray he said: when you pray our heavenly Father may your name be honored, may your kingdom comes, and may your will be done on the Earth as it is in heaven…" His kingdom is all about his ruling, his government in other ways his laws.

In other ways whenever you are praying that prayer that you are always praying you are saying heavenly Father may you be king in the World and may the World follows your own laws and live according to your laws but not according to the will of the devil, Satan who is the enemy of God and his people.

He told his disciples to pray: "Our Father in heaven may your kingdom comes…" and later on He commissioned his followers: Our authority has been given to me in Heaven and in the Earth. Go and make all nations my disciples, teach them my commandments …" in other ways go all over the World and make the Whole world my kingdom because the ruler of the World was judged that is the devil, Satan. Jesus commanded them to teach nations about His commandments. In other words go and discipline the nations. How? by setting up his commandments , his laws because Jesus is the King of kings so he has laws that He wants us to put in place so that all the nations(peoples) he died for willingly must follow just to love him back. And He deserves our love to him! The best and easiest way to make the people his disciples it is to be on the top! No wonder the promise of God to His people is to be the head and not the tail. God knows that once His people are on the top or they are the head therefore they are in control and thus, God Himself is in control through them.

Jesus asked Saul:" Why are you persecuting me?" It means whatever you are doing including leading a nation in the name of Jesus; It is Jesus who is doing that through His believers.

It is written that I will give to my people shepherds after my own heart in other words I will produce; stir up leaders who would rule my people like my servant David.

My beloved the president of Burundi Nkurunziza Peter said one day: **"The glory flows from the top to the low!"** In other words it matters what is in the heart of the leaders. If they are full of the glory of God, then the entire subject will swim in the glory of God! A child always to imitate his father, his parents those on the top of him! It is naturally inculcated in human beings. So go the leaders, so go the nations. All this to tell you why God is looking His people to be heads over nations or be on to in life for them to be the light.

As a scientist I like to observe because I was trained so at school. So One day I observed a behavior of two children brothers that I love. The older One is about 5 years old while the little one is about 3 years old. I called to come to me the little one but he refused at first and then I changed the tactic I knew if I call the older one the other one will follow because the little one always follow the older one. And I succeeded. The little one followed the older one up where I was.

The little one would follow exactly every movement the older brother was doing. Leaders from all over the World watch your behavior because you are where you are to represent Christ Jesus on the earth and you should deputize him well. From where you are on the top, you must reflect his light (the ways or the laws of Jesus the king of kings) to His people.

A good leader who is ruling or leading the people according to the laws of the owner of the Heaven and the Earth Jesus Christ who is Lord of all is the salt of the world and without him the world is bitter.

I am writing this book to empower and to encourage those who are called to govern nations to discipline the nations according to their lover Jesus Christ to be ready and prepare themselves for that noble mission. It is written that I will give to my people shepherds after my own heart in other words I will produce; stir up leaders who would rule my people like my servant David.

Most of people to become leaders of nations or to gain wealth they have to sacrifice their beloved ones according to what I always hear people saying. That is a lie from the devil. As children of God we know that Jesus has already paid the price needed for our peace, our prosperity in short our well –being. You do need to worship the devil in any way to get what you want. Satan will never give you anything good.

The Lord Jesus said that the work of Satan is to steal, to destroy and to kill. Right now if there is any gain you got through occultism I invite to repent and receive Jesus Christ as your Lord and God the savior. The blood our beloved Jesus shed is more precious than any blood you can find.

He is a son of God and whoever who is hidden in His name is greater than those who are used by the darkness. A sin will always make people cheap and weak.

Chapter 6. The World kingdom called "Bethel", a holy nation under one God Jesus Christ and me his King David.

There is a day two brothers wanted to fight each other. News were busy evaluating how many people were going to die because both of two nations have atomic bomb, the massive destruction weapon. These two brother nations I am talking about were India and Pakistan. I prayed to God for them because they are my beloved people. Remember that His majesty Jesus Christ the Word of God told me:

" If you ask me, I will give you the nations; everyone on earth will be yours. You will rule over them with great power and scatter your enemies like broken pieces of pottery." Psalm2 , Good News Bible

I did ask it and received because Jesus our wonderful teacher and Mentor and mighty God taught us that "when you ask anything to God believe that you have received it." I like to practice the Word of God because I want to be among of the wise people who are "those who hear the Word of God and do it." I love to please my wonderful Savior by believing in His Word! I like to have the faith Abraham had in God without wavering because the one who promised is faithful and He is able to perform he says He will do. If his excellence my beloved president Trump can try to keep his word to our beloved great people of America, how more the Lord Jesus Christ who created Trump can keep his word and more than Trump because Jesus is the Almighty God. No one can hinder Him!

Now you understand why I always see all nations as my own people that I love because you cannot pray for someone you do not love. What God has given me no man can refuse it to me! He is the Sovereign God over all His creation! He is faithful in all his promises! Praise the Lord Jesus Christ!

"Lord, please do not allow this war between India and Pakistan because most of them maybe people who fear and love you if they are given a chance to live." That is how I prayed for India and Pakistan.

Did I pray only for Pakistan and India? Oh of course not! I prayed for United States of America (USA) and Iran when there was a high tension between these brother nations that I love as my own people as well.

What was the cause of the tension? The cause was that Iranians want the nuclear weapon America has already. America does not want Iranians to possess what they have. In the same way North Korea wanted the atomic bomb but America do not dream seeing North Korea and

Iranians have the dangerous weapon. It is not only America that has the nuclear arm there are also "India, Pakistan, Israel, China, France, Russia,…".

Those nations have the horrible arm but they do not want others nations to have it. Is it fair? Is it just? I do not think so. You cannot have an arm and refuse other nations not to because as long as you have what you do not want others to have then they will try to have it by all means because they don't feel secure and safe. You all know that the World is not safe as long as we have those weapons between us. It is like fire in our pocket. Anytime they may explode and destroy our dear World.

The time of safety all over the World has come! The God of gods and Lord of lords who redeemed Humanity from the power of Satan is going to abolish bow and sword and battle from the world so that all may lie down in safety (like in Hosea 2:18). Beloved people from all over the world, I have good news assuring you that the time of destroying the weapons has come!

Nations are going to destroy their arms, nuclear weapons,…because all the nations we form now one nation, a holy nation under one King and under one God in the name of Jesus Christ the King of kings and Lord of lords!

There will be no longer a nation fighting against another nation, nor train for war anymore according to what is written in Isaiah2 and **"from the west, people will fear the name of the LORD Jesus Christ and from the rising of the sun, they will revere his glory. For he will come like a pent-up flood that the breath of the LORD drives along." Isaiah59:19, New International Version.**

The Lord has stirred me up through His glorious Word in order of his king David to gather all nations as one nation to show them His glory.

King David was a great king of Israel who many times would ask God the creator of heaven and the earth if he is with him or not. God does speak! He created your mouth, he can speak, He created your ears He can hear, and He created your eyes He can see even where human beings cannot see. No creature can be greater than the creator.

He is ready to protect his king through his Word that is like a fire, The God of all the Earth has chosen me to rule the world his sheep and exalt his glorious law **(Isaiah 42:21)**. He has sent me to make sure that the whole world glorifies him and sing his praise **(Isaiah 42:12)** "

The Lord Jesus Christ will be alone exalted in my time and the idols will totally disappear!"His majesty the mighty God Jesus Christ never dies in vain. He is with me and I will accomplish that through his power. Because my Kingdom, the Whole World will be His Kingdom, His house, Bethel meaning the house of God.

He told me again: don't be afraid, for I am with you. Don't be discouraged, for I am your God. I will strengthen you and help you. I will hold you with my victorious right hand. See, all your angry enemies lie there, confused and humiliated. Anyone who opposes you will die and come to nothing. You will look in vain for those who tried to conquer you. Those who attack you will come to nothing. For I hold you by your right hand, I the lord your God. I say to you, don't be afraid. I am here to help you! **Isaiah 41-13.**

Moreover, Jesus the Messiah told me:" I am the one who comforts you. So why are you afraid of mere humans who wither like the grass and disappear? Yet you have forgotten the Lord your Creator who stretched out the sky like a canopy and laid the foundations of the earth. Will you remain in constant dread of human oppressors? Will you continue to fear the anger 6f your enemies? Where is their fury and anger now?"**Isaiah51:12-13.**

The Lord will be called the God of all the earth. How Jesus Christ the creator of all universe is He going to do that? You may ask yourself.

Let me remind you something in the book (the holy bible) of the prophet of God ezekiel34. In the time of kings in Israel the shepherds (kings or leaders) stopped taking care of the flock (the people) of God, the creator of universe. In that time the only true God called in that time "I am" was only the God of Israel the only nation in the whole world that was considered by God like His people. The leaders of Israel were taking care for themselves and left the sheep, his people to starve and rule them with harshness and cruelty instead. God said:" I will remove those leaders from tending my flock so that the shepherds can no longer feed themselves. I will rescue my flock from their mouth.

Moreover in the same chapter God said:" I myself will tend my sheep and have them lie down. I will search for my sheep and look after them." And again God said:" I myself will judge between the fat sheep and the lean sheep (meaning between the rich and the poor or the strong and the weak)." The question is:"Is the God who is Spirit going to judge directly the people in the land of Israel? Oh no. He has someone; God has prepared someone who will be ruling in His name. A human being whose heart is after God. A man who has the Spirit of God in him.

That is why God said in the same chapter ezekiel34:23:" I will set over them one shepherd who is like my servant David. He will feed them and be a shepherd to them. And I the Lord will be their God, and my servant David will be a prince among my people. I the Lord have spoken."

The prophet Ezekiel was not alive in the time David king was ruling Israel. But God is using him to prophecy about the future, our time. The plan of God never dies. In his mind is to restore the throne of David through Jesus Christ. The throne of David is the throne of God. The kingdom of David is the kingdom of God because David ruled in the name of God. He was a king of God chosen to rule. He was his anointed one.

The mind of God was not only to be called the God of the only one nation Israel. His plan is to be called the God of all the earth. But how?

In The book of John chapter 1:29-30 we read:" The next day John the Baptist saw Jesus coming toward him to be baptized and said:" Look! The Lamb of God who takes away the sin of the world! He is the one I was talking about when I said,' A man is coming after me who am far greater than I am, for he existed long before me."

Do you see? When Jesus came in the very world he created (John1:10) he came to save the entire world and not the only nation of Israel. Why Jesus is called the Everlasting father? Because during the travail of his soul when he was suffering for the world and die for the sin of the World to justify them the world became his descendant, his seed, his offspring(from Isaiah53:10-11) in order words, Jesus became the Father or the source of the World. And because Jesus was a descendant of David so his descendants became also descendants of David, descendants of Jacob, a descendant of Abraham. For that I can declare boldly that I am a son of Abraham, a son of David through Christ Jesus.

Remember that God said in Ezekiel 34:20:" I myself will judge between the fat sheep and the lean one." But we saw also that God said**:" I give them a shepherd who is like my servant David to judge them**. In the book of **zechariah14:8** God said that the least of his people will become as mighty as King David. And in the same verse it is written that the descendants of David will lead the people like God himself, like an angel of God. David was leading the nation of Israel in his time like God himself, like angel of God. That is why David to judge the nation was doing it like God himself, like angel of God.

In psalm82:8. It is written: "Arise o God, judge the earth for thou shalt inherit all nations." Remember that God used to call only the nation of Israel his inheritance. It does not mean that all the people of Israel were doing his laws but they were still called his people. Sometimes God would punish those who committed sins and some of those with sins would be killed by God as punishment.

But in that psalm82:8, God is going to judge the earth because now all the nations are his inheritance and be called the God of all the earth because he redeemed all the earth.

In Isaiah 54:5 we read: For thy maker is thin husband; the Lord of hosts is his name; and thy redeemer the holy one of Israel; **the God of the whole earth** shall be called. King James Version.

Now the holy one of Israel is now the holy one of all the earth who is Jesus who is holy and true and "was slaughtered and his blood has ransomed people of God from every tribe and language and people and nation." Revelation5:9.

Jesus Christ is the one called the king of kings and lord of lords in revelation. In psalm136:2-3 It is written: "Give thanks to the God of gods and the Lord of lords. So Jesus who is the Lord of lords is also the God of gods. He is the same God who saved Israel in Egypt where He killed the firstborn for the King of Egypt Pharaoh to release his people of Israel.

Jesus is the same God who was with David in Old Testament and He is the one who is with me in this last days.

He has sent me like His son David to lead the world like God himself like an angel of God to judge the entire world his inheritance in the name of the Lord Jesus Christ the wonderful savior forever. The Lord Jesus is going to judge and save the entire world through me his king in the same way He judged and saved the nation of Israel through his king David in the Old Testament. Jesus is the same today, yesterday and forever.

In the same way people loved God in the time of David it is going to be the same thing in my time. People from all over the world will love Jesus easily because my assignment is to remove obstacle. When David ruled the nation of Israel in his time the glory of God filled all the nation of Israel. Likewise the glory of God that I have received as his king David in my time is going to fill all the earth the great nation.

The entire world is going to be the holy nation of Jesus Christ our only true God! The Lord Jesus has sent to fulfill his word written in the bible the book of Zechariah14:9:"**The Lord will be king over all the earth! On that day there will be one Lord (Jesus Christ our Savior and God our maker)-his name alone will be worshiped.**" How? Through me His king in the same way Jesus was the king of Israel through David!

The time of persecution to the lover our Lord Jesus is over! Those who died while taking the gospel in other nations did not die in vain like the people who came from Sweden up to Burundi. Some of those missionaries died in Congo. They are those who us the gospel and found a church called the Pentecostal church. Those missionaries received the gospel Holy Spirit that they brought us from America. That is why I love the Swedish nation and America without forgetting the nation of Israel the source of Lord Jesus Christ.

I am gathering all nations together and assemble the peoples of the world into one holy nation of our beloved Jesus Christ the almighty God according to command of God written in Isaiah43:9:"**Gather the nations together! Assemble the peoples of the world!**"; "**For I know their works and their thoughts; the time is coming to gather all nations and tongues. And they shall come and see My glory**. Isaiah 66:18.

Through his death, the Lord Jesus removed the sin of the world and became the God of the World the Father of the World and not only the God of Israel the small nation.

Bethel which means "**the house of God**", the world nation is a kingdom because Jesus Christ our Father or our source of the everlasting life is King.

Bethel will be called a **righteous city**, a **faithful city** because the whole world is immersed in the righteousness of God! It will be like "World without sea" because we are **one world, one people one family**!

I have come in the name of Jesus like his king David to restore the "throne of David", the "Throne of God" because the kingdom is the Lord's! I have come to establish the kingdom of

God here on earth in the name of Jesus Christ who is the new Adam for the glory of our heavenly father.

The capital of this great world kingdom is **New York** like the "**New Jerusalem**"! The whole world is governed by his king helped by 24 lords who rule in the name of Jesus Christ who is the king of kings and Lord of lords.

We are going to use English like the official language while different local languages are there like what is in Zambia. English is an official language but we have a lot of local languages due to different tribes and build Zambia as one people that love each other despite their many differences.

After the king, they are 24 lords with that are in charge of different 6 continents represented by 4 lords from every continent. 1th from Northern area, 2nd from Southern area; 3rd from Eastern area and 4th from Western area:

-**4from Africa;**

-**4from Europe;**

-**4from Asia;**

-**4from North America;**

-**4from South America;**

-**4from Australia /Oceania.**

Every nation will ruled by a governor and a vice governor.

Before any meeting, people will be singing:" **Holy, holy, holy is the Lord God Almighty Jesus Christ who is the same yesterday, today and forever! The whole earth is full of his glory!"**

After that, all the leaders including the king will bow down and worship Jesus Christ, **the King of kings and Lord of lords** the one who lives forever and died for us because He loved us in order to save us from the dark hand of the devil Satan. Then the people will say: **"You are worthy our Lord and God to receive glory, honor and power for you created all things, and by your will they were created and have their being!"**

The law and the word of God shall come from the "new Jerusalem".

I call all the nations (Presidents, ministers, kings, queens, governors, companies, people from different field of life from all over the world, Africa, America, Asia, Oceania, Islands,…) to join in me in this very noble cause for our Lord and God Jesus Christ and for our world. **Remember it is said:" Success to David and SUCCESS TO THOSE WHO HELP HIM!**

There will be rapid response (success) to those who help me and quick bad consequences to those who plan against me. Any plan against me will be immediately destroyed with serious plague. If mere humans know how to protect their presidents, how more our God can make sure that his king who has come in his name cannot be touched everywhere!

It is written as serious warning:"Therefore, you king (leaders from all over the world), be wise; be warned, you rulers of the earth. [11] Serve the Lord with fear and celebrate his rule with trembling.

¹² Kiss his son(an act of submission or obedience), or he will be angry and your way will lead to your destruction, for his wrath can flare up in a moment. Blessed are all who take refuge in him." Psalm2:10-12, New International Version!

The time of the Kingdom of God has come! "This is the purpose that is purposed upon the whole earth; and this is the hand that is stretched out upon all the nations. For Jehovah of hosts hath purposed, and who shall annul it? And his hand is stretched out, and who shall turn it back? Isaiah 14:26-27. American Standard Version.

Let all the nations praise the Lord Jesus Christ forever! Let heavens dance for him with joy and all creation bows down to the Lord God in worship! Hallelujah!

Praise be to the Lord God Jesus Christ, the God of all the earth, who alone does marvelous deeds.

Praise be to his glorious name forever; may the whole earth be filled with his glory. Amen and Amen.

God bless our all nations, I love you all and I pray for you! May prosperity, peace and righteousness of God and good health be found all over the world and all over the Universe!

One world one nation under one God, Jesus Christ

www.ingramcontent.com/pod-product-compliance
Lightning Source LLC
Chambersburg PA
CBHW072242260726
48657CB00001BA/278